Girl's World

Girl's World

Twenty-One Sewing Projects
to Make for *Little Girls*

JENNIFER PAGANELLI
CREATOR OF SIS BOOM FABRICS

WITH
DOLIN O'SHEA

PHOTOGRAPHS BY
TIM GEANEY

CHRONICLE BOOKS
SAN FRANCISCO

Library of Congress Cataloging-in-Publication Data
Paganelli, Jennifer.
Girl's world: twenty-one sewing projects to make for little girls /
Jennifer Paganelli with Dolin O'Shea ; photographs by Tim Geaney.
p. cm.
ISBN: 978-0-8118-7444-1
1. Textile crafts. 2. Girls' clothing. I. O'Shea, Dolin. II. Title.
TT705.P25 2011 | 746—dc22 | 2010014610

CPE Stick-It Felt is a registered trademark of CPE Felt Company.
Dritz is a registered trademark of Prym Consumer USA Inc.
Elmer's is a registered trademark of Elmer's Products, Inc.
Homasote is a registered trademark of Homasote Co.
Hug Snug is a registered trademark of Lawrence Chiff Silk Mills, Inc.
HTC Ultra Firm is a registered trademark of HTC-Retail, Inc.
Mod Podge is a registered trademark of Plaid Enterprises, Inc.
Thermolam Plus is a registered trademark of Stacy Fabrics Corp.

Manufactured in China
DESIGN BY DESIGN ARMY

1 3 5 7 9 10 8 6 4 2

CHRONICLE BOOKS LLC
680 Second Street
San Francisco, California 94107
www.chroniclebooks.com

To my amazing husband, **PETER**, for allowing me to overrun our lives—and our home—with glitter, flowers, fabric, a big chubby Labradoodle named George; and to my two extraordinary children who are on their way to doing great things. I love you, **MATT** and **KATE**.

To longtime friends **TIM** and **NANCY GEANEY**, who continue to help celebrate the small successes and always shine a light of hope in my direction. I love you both.

To **MARY**, my witty and good-natured friend with a gift for styling the most amazing rooms. You make it so easy.

To **DOLIN O'SHEA**, who jumped right in and made it all happen. I couldn't have imagined a more perfect union.

And to **CARLA HAGEMAN CRIM**, who had our backs and whose love and loyalty bring me joy.

To **MY CLOSE GIRLFRIENDS**, who help me to focus on abundance and the good things in life. They always bring me perspective and I love them for that. You know who you are.

To **MARITZA**, the upholstering magician and incredible spirit, and to **BETTYANN**, my friend and seamstress who spins it all into gold.

To **MADDIE** and **DANA**, for their goodness.

To **THE SIS BOOM FANS**, who keep my inbox overflowing and my heart full.

To **JOHN** and **DANDERS**, and our extended family on both sides who can't get enough Sis Boom, all my love.

To my literary agent, **JILL COHEN**, who as if by some divine design was able to bring Sis Boom to you, the reader, in the most beautiful of ways. Jill, your friendship and passion means the world to me!

To **FREESPIRIT FABRIC**, for providing oodles of Sis Boom fabric for the book. And to my friends at **CHRONICLE**, who were so patient with this first-time author and made a book that surpassed my wildest dreams.

And to **MY FAMILY**:

To my **PARENTS**, for taking us to the U.S. Virgin Islands when I was eleven years old and exposing me to the tropical beauty of St. Croix.

To my mom, **PATRICIA**, who said I could be whatever I wanted to be, and believed it. She taught me the everyday beauty of island living. I love you!

To my siblings **BRIDGET**, **MOLLY**, **SHANA**, and **MEGHAN** and my womb mate, **JAMES**—you bring out the best in me.

To **BETH**, for her beautiful spirit, friendship, and guidance.

And finally to **BILL W.**, for a better way.

Contents

Welcome to Girl's World!

AS A FABRIC DESIGNER FOR MY COMPANY SIS BOOM, I get all sorts of inspiration from the girls in my life. Their energy, imagination, and joy spur me on to come up with playful patterns and exuberant color combinations. In this book I hope to share a bit of that Sis Boom inspiration. You'll find my favorite projects and something for every skill level—from the simple and elegant "Sophie Glittered Apron" *(page 71)* to the more complex and sophisticated "Josie Dress" *(page 51)*. Although the projects in this book are designed for girls ages two to fourteen, there is no age limit on the *Girl's World* style. I've even included a few projects that don't require any sewing but are so much fun to make, like the "Hadley Headband" *(page 91)* and "Olivia Floral Lamp Shade" *(page 149)*. Close to my heart are the "Girls' 'Ambassador of Goodwill' Badges" *(page 107)*; words of encouragement can effect great change and build self-esteem. These badges are a cinch to put together and make for lovely party favors.

As a mom, and having grown up in a creative, supportive, and fun environment, I know first-hand how important it is to foster girls' creativity and imagination. Encourage the girls in your life to help with these projects. Let them pick out the fabric for a new dress, or teach them how to sew by making one of the projects in this book. These handmade items create opportunities for lasting memories—a tea party with favorite stuffed animals, getting dizzy twirling around in a ballet skirt, picnicking on a pretty handmade quilt. It's a joy to sew for your little girl knowing that the love you put into that stuffed animal, ballet skirt, or quilt will make those memories even more cherished.

At the front of the book you'll find lots of helpful information on how to get started. I've included tips on stocking your sewing basket, along with a detailed "Glossary of Techniques" *(page 20)*. The pocket attached to the front cover holds the pattern pieces. Diagrams and photographs throughout will help you get picture-perfect results.

This book was so exciting to put together, and I couldn't have done it without the encouragement and love from so many. I am moved by all of you who have wished me well, who have loved me and my work. I will continue to be inspired by you. Now, go and make something pretty!

Getting Started

I DON'T KNOW ABOUT YOU, but I have many fond memories of my grandmother's sewing basket. It was a treasure trove of all sorts of items that were a mystery to me at the time. In this section I suggest some basic items so you can stock your own sewing basket and craft cabinet. This is just a guideline; there are many more supplies that you may find useful. Also in this section, you'll find how-to information for the sewing techniques used in the projects in this book.

Sewing Basket Basics

HERE ARE THE ITEMS YOU WILL NEED TO KEEP IN YOUR SEWING BASKET:

* Assortment of hand-sewing needles
* Clear grid ruler
* Iron and ironing board
* Scissors (for use only on fabric)
* Seam ripper
* Sewing machine
* Small gauge string or crochet cotton
* Straight pins
* Tape measure
* Turning tool (or the tip of a pair of scissors or knitting needle)
* Water-soluble fabric marker and/or chalk pencil

THE ITEMS BELOW ARE NOT NECESSARY, BUT THEY ARE NICE TO HAVE AROUND:

* Cutting mat
* Rotary cutter
* Tracing paper (This is very handy if you want to use the patterns provided in multiple sizes. Just trace the size/s you want on the tracing paper and cut out to use as the sewing pattern.)

Craft Cabinet Basics

* Toolbox outfitted with basic equipment (including hammer, screwdrivers and power drill with bits)
* Dual-temperature glue gun
* Glue sticks
* Scissors (for use on paper)
* White all-purpose glue (such as Elmer's)

General Notes for All Projects

* Preshrink all fabrics before using. To preshrink fabric, wash, dry, and press fabric according to manufacturer's instructions.

* Feel free to be creative when choosing fabrics. You can use one, two, or more different fabrics on one project. In each project, the yardage requirements are broken down for each component; for instance, a dress might require materials for the bodice, skirt, and perhaps a sash or binding, and all are listed separately. If you want to make the bodice, skirt, and sash out of the same fabric, then add up those yardage requirements to determine the total yardage needed.

* All pattern pieces and cut measurement dimensions include seam allowances. Seam allowance amounts are given in the instructions of each project.

* Before you start a project, have all necessary materials, sewing basket items, and craft cabinet items for that project ready and available for use.

* At the beginning and ending of each seam, backstitch a few stitches to secure the seam and make sure it doesn't come undone. The only time that you don't want to backstitch is when you're basting.

* Almost all of the sewing in this book is done with a sewing machine, unless otherwise stated. There are a few projects that require small amounts of hand sewing to finish them off; the instructions for these projects will let you know when to use a specific hand-sewing technique.

* For all the sewing projects that require pressing, please be sure to follow the iron and/or fabric manufacturer's recommendations for temperature.

* When cutting out the various projects, please be sure to use the appropriate type of scissors for the material you are cutting. Cut fabric with only your fabric scissors and cut paper with only your paper scissors. Paper dulls the scissors blades very quickly, so it is best to have different scissors for each of your cutting needs.

* Please use caution when using a dual-temperature glue gun and follow the manufacturer's instructions for use.

* Make sure to let glue dry before proceeding to the next step and before using or wearing the item.

Sizing

SIZE AND APPROXIMATE AGE	X-SMALL 2-3	SMALL 4-5	MEDIUM 6-7	LARGE 8-10	X-LARGE 12-14
Height	33–39 in/ 84–99 cm	39–45 in/ 99–114 cm	45–51 in/ 114–130 cm	51–57 in/ 130–145 cm	57–62 in/ 145–157 cm
Chest	20–22 in/ 51–56 cm	22½–24½ in/ 57–62 cm	25–26½ in/ 63.5–67 cm	27–29 in/ 68.5–73.5 cm	29–32 in/ 73.5–81 cm
Waist	20–21 in/ 51–53 cm	21–22 in/ 53–56 cm	20½–23 in/ 52–58.5 cm	21½–24 in/ 54.5–61 cm	23½–26 in/ 60–66 cm
Hip	20¾–22¾ in/ 53–58 cm	23½–25½ in/ 60–65 cm	26–27½ in/ 66–70 cm	28–30 in/ 71–76 cm	31–33 in/ 79–84 cm
Head Circumference	19½–20 in/ 49.5–51 cm	20–20½ in/ 51–52 cm	20½–21 in/ 52–53 cm	21–21½ in/ 53–54.5 cm	21½–22 in/ 54.5–56 cm
Weight	30–36 lbs/ 13.5–16.5 kg	36–46 lbs/ 16.5–21 kg	44–55 lbs/ 20–25 kg	54–74 lbs/ 24.5–33.5 kg	75–95 lbs/ 34–43 kg

Glossary of Techniques

BACKSTITCH

Backstitching is done at the start and end of each seam you sew. When beginning a seam, sew a few stitches forward, and then press the reverse button on your sewing machine to go back over the first stitches made. Continue sewing forward until the end of the seam, and then sew a few stitches in reverse to go over the last few stitches made. The backstitch is also a hand-sewing stitch. For more information, please see "Hand-Tied Quilting" *(page 27)*.

BASTE

Basting is a temporary stitch that can be done by machine or by hand and is usually removed when an item is completed. It comes in very handy when you need to keep things in place before stitching them together permanently. To baste by machine, set the straight stitch length to the longest setting and sew as usual. *Most of the basting done in this book will be by machine.* The only project in the book that you may want to baste by hand is the "Genevieve Patchwork Square Quilt" *(page 141)*. To baste by hand, do a simple running stitch, but with longer stitches than usual. For more information, please see "Running Stitch" *(page 27)*.

BIAS

The bias grain runs diagonally, at a 45-degree angle, between the length and cross grain of the fabric. To cut on the bias, make sure the grain line on the pattern is placed at a 45-degree angle to the selvage. When fabric is cut on the bias it becomes slightly stretchy and has a bit of give.

BINDING

Binding is made with strips of fabric that are used to encase the raw edges of a project, creating a finished edge. The binding strips can be cut on the cross grain or on the bias. The strips cut on the cross grain are used on straight edges. The strips cut on the bias are used on curved edges, such as a neckline or an armhole. Binding strips may be folded in different ways to achieve different effects. There are three different types of folded binding used in this book:

1. *Single-fold binding:* This binding has a fold along each long edge of the binding. It is used to finish edges and is only seen from the **one** side of the project. This type of binding is used on "Mary's Fancy Sash Dress" *(page 35)* and will only be seen on the **wrong** side of the bodice. *(See illustration.)*

2. *Double-fold binding:* This binding has the same two folds as for the single-fold binding, but in double-fold binding it is then folded again, lengthwise, down the center, aligning both of the folded edges. This binding is used to encase raw edges and is seen on both sides of the project. This type of binding is used on the "Bridget Banner with Pom-Poms" *(page 117)* and the "Happy Birthday Banner" *(page 165)*. *(See illustration.)*

✳ BINDING ✳

TYPES OF BINDING

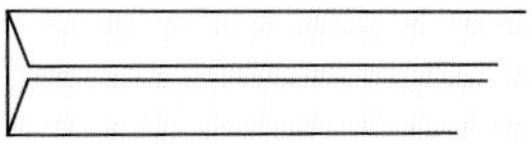

Single-fold binding

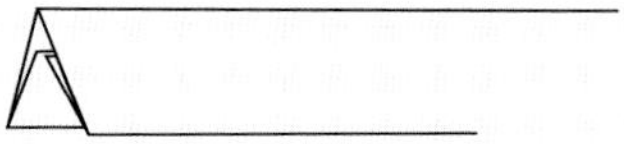

Double-fold binding

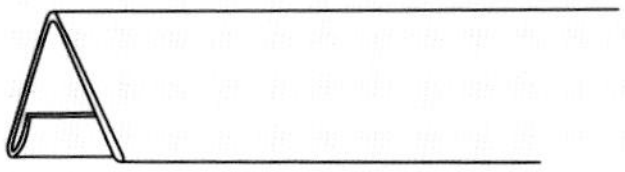

Double-layer binding

CUTTING BIAS BINDING STRIPS

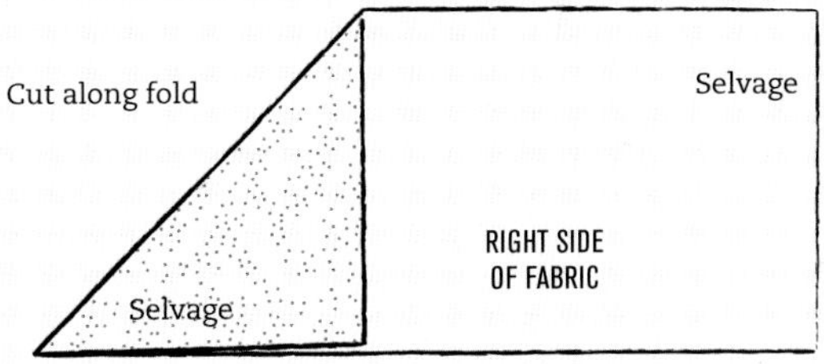

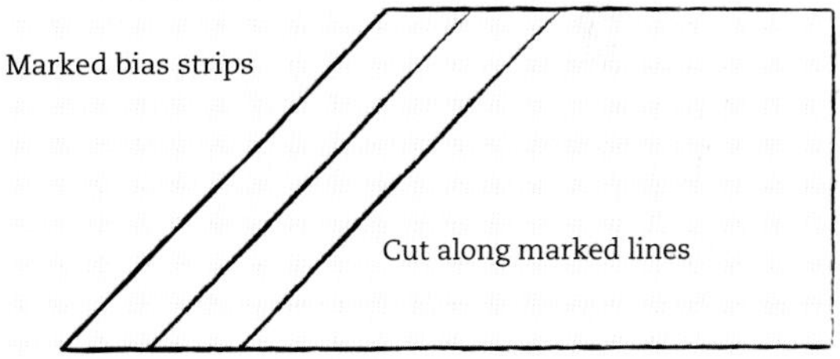

Cut along fold

Selvage

Selvage

RIGHT SIDE
OF FABRIC

Marked bias strips

Cut along marked lines

CUTTING CROSS-GRAIN BINDING STRIPS

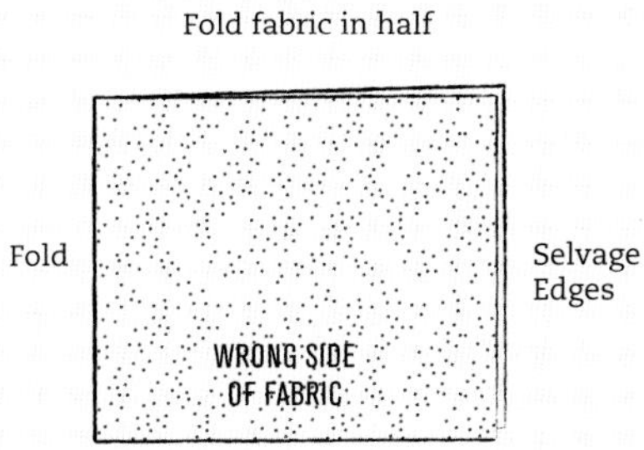

Fold fabric in half

Fold

Selvage
Edges

WRONG SIDE
OF FABRIC

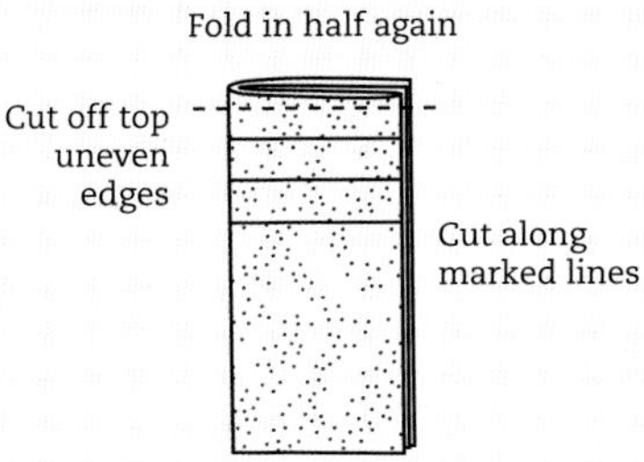

Fold in half again

Cut off top
uneven
edges

Cut along
marked lines

JOINING BINDING STRIPS

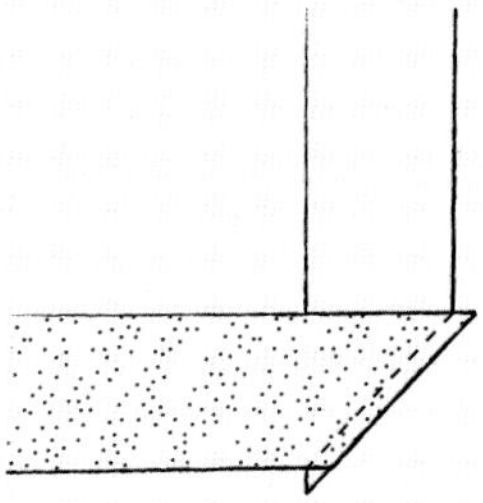

3. *Double-layer binding:* This binding is folded in half lengthwise, aligning the long raw edges with **wrong** sides together. The raw edges are sewn along the edge of the project, and the entire binding is folded to the **wrong** side, so that it encases the raw edges, and then stitched down on the **wrong** side of the project. This binding is more durable and is used mainly to bind the edges of quilts, like the "Genevieve Patchwork Square Quilt" *(page 141)*. *(See illustration on page 21.)*

Please note that each of the three types of binding can be either cut on the cross grain or the bias grain. The instructions for each project will specify on which grain to cut the binding strips and how they should be folded.

INSTRUCTIONS FOR CUTTING BINDING STRIPS

On the bias: Lay fabric **right**-side up on a flat surface. Fold one corner over, **right** sides together, aligning the selvage edge with the cut edge of fabric. Carefully cut along the diagonal fold. Beginning at the cut edge, measure the width specified in the project and draw a line with marker or chalk. Continue measuring from each line until you have enough strips for the length of binding called for in the instructions. Cut the strips along the drawn lines. *(See illustration on page 21.)*

On the cross grain: Lay fabric **right**-side up on a flat surface. Fold fabric in half, with **right** sides together, aligning the selvage edges. Fold in half again, aligning fold with selvage. Square off top raw edge by cutting straight across at a 90-degree angle from the selvage. Beginning at the squared-off edge, measure the width specified in the project and draw a line. Continue measuring over from each line until you have enough strips for the length of binding called for in the instructions. Cut the strips along the drawn lines, and then cut each end at a 45-degree angle, making sure to remove the selvage edges. *(See illustration on page 21.)*

INSTRUCTIONS FOR JOINING BINDING STRIPS

Lay strips perpendicular to each other, with **right** sides together, aligning short ends. Sew ends together using a ¼-in/6-mm seam allowance. Press seam open and trim off the small points of fabric that extend past the seam. After all the binding strips are joined, you will need to fold and press the joined strip into one of the three types of binding (mentioned above). Each of the projects that uses binding will specify which type to use. *(See illustration on page 21.)*

CLIP SEAM ALLOWANCE

Clipping the seam allowance on curved seams makes it possible for the seam allowance to lay flat on the **wrong** side and creates a smoothly shaped seam on the **right** side. After sewing a curved seam, using very sharp scissors make small cuts in the seam allowance; be very careful to not cut the stitching of the seam. On a sharply curved seam you will need to make more clips than you would on a slightly curved seam.

CUT ON THE FOLD

Some pattern pieces represent only half of the complete piece; you are meant to fold your fabric before cutting, so that you will have a full-size piece after cutting. If a pattern piece instructs to cut on the fold, fold the fabric and place the edge of the pattern marked "Place on the fold" along the folded edge. Cut around the outer edges. When you finish cutting and unfold the piece, each half of the piece will be a mirror image of the other half.

EDGE STITCH

Edge stitching is a form of topstitching that is done very close to an edge or a seam—usually ¹⁄₁₆ in/ 2 mm to ⅛ in/3 mm from the edge or seam. For more information, please see "Topstitch" *(page 28)*.

FINISHING EDGES

You'll want to finish the edges on any seam allowance that's exposed on the inside of a garment or on an item that will be washed frequently; it's necessary for a clean, finished look and to keep the edges of the fabric from fraying. There are many ways to finish the edges of the seam allowance, but the three most common methods are serging with a serger, zigzagging with a sewing machine, and trimming with pinking shears. *(See illustration.)*

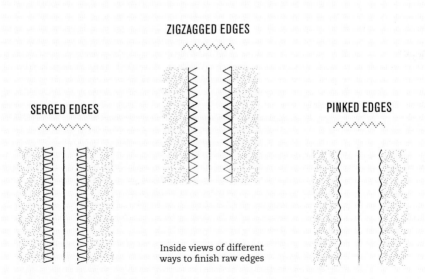

❋ TYPES OF FINISHED EDGES ❋

ZIGZAGGED EDGES

SERGED EDGES

PINKED EDGES

Inside views of different ways to finish raw edges

FREE-MOTION QUILTING

Free-motion quilting is one of the many ways to sew the three layers of a quilt together. In order to do free-motion quilting, you will need to make sure that your sewing machine can drop the feed dogs and has a darning foot. With the feed dogs dropped, you're able to move the fabric in any direction, not just forward and backward as in regular sewing. Because you can move the fabric in any direction, you can "draw" or stitch any type of design that you wish. The "Genevieve Patchwork Square Quilt" *(page 141)* has a free-motion pattern throughout the entire quilt. It's a lot of fun, but it can take some practice. Try it out on some fabric scraps first, to get a feel for it. If you need more information, look online for some great tutorials and resources.

GATHERING

Gathering is done when you want to attach a larger piece of fabric to a smaller piece—for instance, when you sew a full skirt into a fitted bodice. Gathering can also be used to create visual interest and draw attention to a certain area, like a neckline or a sleeve, and to make ruffles. There are two methods of creating gathers used in this book, each suited for the particular amount of gathering needed for a project. The instructions for each project will specify which method to use.

METHOD ONE

This method works best when gathering smaller areas, like along a neckline. Run 1 row of basting stitches ⅛ in/3 mm above, and another row of basting stitches ⅛ in/33 mm below, the called-for seam allowance in the section that is to be gathered. For example, if the seam allowance is ⅝ in/16 mm, you would stitch a basting seam at ½ in/12 mm from the raw edge and another ¾ in/2 cm from the raw edge. After stitching the 2 rows of basting stitches, pick up only the bobbin threads and gently pull; the fabric will gather up along your stitches. To help yourself remember which threads are the bobbin threads, use a different color thread for the bobbin. Once the piece has the required amount of gathering, pin it to the piece to which it will be sewn, according to the pattern and/or instructions. Distribute the gathers evenly, and then sew the 2 pieces together. After sewing the pieces together, you will need to remove the visible basting threads with a seam ripper. *(See illustration.)*

METHOD TWO

This method is best used when you need to gather a larger area, like a skirt to be attached to a bodice. This method has more-durable results; there is no chance of breaking the bobbin threads as there is with Method One when used on larger areas. You'll need some nonstretchy, small-gauge string (crochet cotton works really well) and zigzag stitch capabilities on your sewing machine. Set the zigzag stitch width to the widest setting and the zigzag length to the longest setting (as for basting). Lay the string on the fabric and center it beneath the presser foot. You'll want the zigzag stitching to be placed ¼ in/6 mm closer to the raw edge than the called-for seam allowance. For example, if the seam allowance is ⅝ in/16 mm, work the zigzag stitch ⅜ in/1 cm from the raw edge, being careful to keep the string centered under the stitching; you don't want it to get caught by the needle. After working the zigzag stitch over the string, pin the soon-to-be-gathered piece to the piece to which it will be sewn according to the instructions, aligning at necessary points or seams. If you're going to gather a skirt

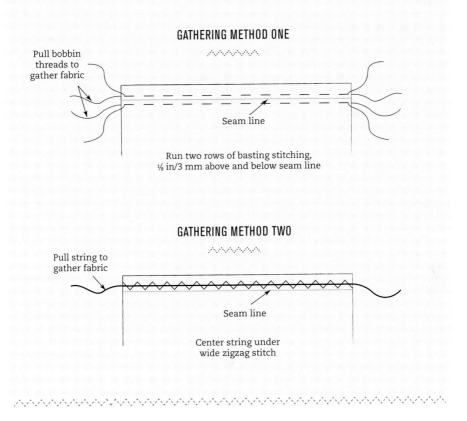

GATHERING METHOD ONE

Pull bobbin threads to gather fabric

Seam line

Run two rows of basting stitching,
⅛ in/3 mm above and below seam line

GATHERING METHOD TWO

Pull string to gather fabric

Seam line

Center string under wide zigzag stitch

into a bodice, you'll want to align and pin at the side seams, and at the center front and center back. Then, pick up the string ends and gently start pulling. Pull until gathered to the correct size, distributing gathers evenly, and pin in place. Sew the pieces together, making sure to not catch the string in the stitching. Once the pieces are sewn together, you should be able to pull the string out entirely. Since the zigzag stitches are on the seam allowance, and not seen from the **right** side, it's up to you whether or not you want to remove them with a seam ripper. *(See illustration.)*

GRAIN OF FABRIC

The grain of the fabric is the direction of the woven threads that make up fabric. Length grain runs the length of the fabric, from cut edge to cut edge. Cross grain runs the width of the fabric, from selvage edge to selvage edge. The bias grain runs diagonally across the length and cross grain (see "Bias," page 20). All pattern pieces in this book are marked with a grain line. This line is there to help you align the pattern piece correctly on the fabric grain. All the pattern grain lines should be aligned along the length grain, unless otherwise noted in the instructions.

❋ HAND-TIED QUILTING ❋

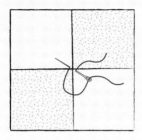

At each interstection take
a small backstitch

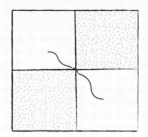

Tie ends into a knot
over the backstitch

❋ RUNNING STITCH ❋

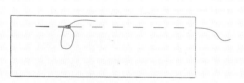

Running stitch as used
when basting by hand

❋ SLIP STITCH ❋

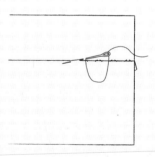

Slip stitch by hand

HAND-TIED QUILTING

Hand tying is a great way to quickly finish a quilt. It's one of the many ways you can quilt the "Genevieve Patchwork Square Quilt" *(page 141)*. You will need a hand-sewing needle and some embroidery floss. With the **right** side of the quilt facing up and the quilt sandwich assembled, take a small backstitch at each intersection between squares. Cut floss, leaving about a 2-in/5-cm tail of floss at each side of the backstitch. Tie the tails in a knot and trim the tails so they're even. *(See illustration.)*

NOTCHES

Notches are the small triangular markings on the cutting lines on the pattern pieces. They're used as a guide for matching up seams and for placement of items along the seam (for example, they might show where to place gathers or straps).

PIVOT

Pivoting is used to change direction in sewing: to turn a corner or continue the stitching in a different direction. To pivot, you simply stop stitching, with the needle in the down position; this will hold the fabric in place. Then raise the presser foot and rotate the fabric in the direction you want to sew. Drop the presser foot and continue sewing.

RUNNING STITCH

A running stitch is one of the most basic hand stitches you can do. It isn't a particularly strong stitch, so it is best suited to use as basting. To do a running stitch, insert the needle into the fabric and then pull back up through fabric at regular intervals. *(See illustration.)*

SEAM ALLOWANCE

The seam allowance is the area of fabric between the sewn seam and the raw edge. The seam allowance can be pressed to one side or the other, or it can be pressed open. See individual project instructions for the recommended pressing direction of the seam allowance.

SLIP STITCH

The slip stitch is a hand-sewing stitch that is nearly invisible. It is perfect for closing up an opening, such as on "George the Puppy" *(page 137)* and the "Willow Small Pillow with Pom-Poms" *(page 131)*. It's also used for attaching a folded edge to a single layer of fabric, as on the "Genevieve Patchwork Square Quilt" *(page 141)* when the binding is sewn to the back of the quilt. To slip stitch, working from right to left, insert the needle into the top fabric and make a tiny stitch. Then insert the needle into the fold on the bottom fabric, and bring the needle back up through the fold about ¼ in/6 mm away from where it was inserted. *(See illustration.)*

STITCH IN THE DITCH

Stitching in the ditch is done by sewing directly in the groove formed by a seam. This technique can be used to sew the layers of the "Genevieve Patchwork Square Quilt" *(page 141)* together.

TRIM CORNERS

Trimming off the corners reduces the amount of excess seam allowance that is inside a seam. To trim the excess seam allowance off, simply cut off the seam allowance close to the seam, being careful not to cut into the seam. When the project is turned **right**-side out, the corners will now be sharper and easier to push out.

TOPSTITCH

Topstitching is an additional row or rows of stitching worked near a seam, using your sewing machine. Topstitching should be done with the project **right**-side up, so you can be sure that the stitching is straight and parallel to the seam. You will also want to be sure that the seam allowance, on the **wrong** side, is caught in the topstitching. Topstitching adds a decorative touch and some extra strength to a seam. The instructions in each project will specify how far the topstitching should be placed from the seam.

UNDER STITCH

Under stitching is used on the inside of a project. It helps to keep seam allowances and linings in place, but it is not visible on the **right** side of a project. To under stitch, press the seam allowance in the direction specified in the project instructions, and then stitch on the side of the seam allowance, very close to the seam line. This technique is used on the "Josie Dress" *(page 51)*. *(See illustration.)*

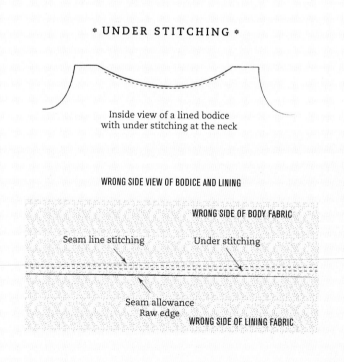

✳ UNDER STITCHING ✳

Inside view of a lined bodice
with under stitching at the neck

WRONG SIDE VIEW OF BODICE AND LINING

WRONG SIDE OF BODY FABRIC

Seam line stitching   Under stitching

Seam allowance
Raw edge   WRONG SIDE OF LINING FABRIC

Dress-up

· № 1 ·

Mary's Fancy Sash Dress

Here's a sweet, old-fashioned dress with a timeless quality.
The wonderful sash adds a bit of frivolity, but the elastic at the
back makes it comfy enough for everyday wear. Feel free to get
creative with fabrics—mix and match to your heart's content.
You can use two or three different fabrics on this dress.

FINISHED SIZE OF DRESS ❋ XS, S, M, L, AND XL

Materials

1 Printed mid-weight cotton fabric (45 in/114 cm wide):

SIZE	XS	S	M	L	XL
Bodice	⅜ yd/ 35 cm	⅜ yd/ 35 cm	⅜ yd/ 35 cm	⅜ yd/ 35 cm	½ yd/ 45 cm
Skirt	1⅛ yd/ 1.1 m	1¼ yd/ 1.2 m	1½ yd/ 1.4 m	1⅝ yd/ 1.5 m	1¾ yd/ 1.6 m
Sash and Bias Tape*	⅝ yd/ 60 cm	⅝ yd/ 60 cm	⅝ yd/ 60 cm	⅝ yd/ 60 cm	⅝ yd/ 60 cm

* If you don't want to make your own bias tape, purchase 1 package of premade ½-in/12-mm single-fold bias tape.

2 Elastic (¼ in/6 mm wide):

SIZE	XS	S	M	L	XL
Cut Elastic Length	7 in/ 18 cm	8 in/ 20 cm	9 in/ 23 cm	10 in/ 25.5 cm	11 in/ 28 cm

3 Coordinating thread

FROM THE SEWING BASKET:

❋ Scissors (for use with paper and fabric)

❋ Tracing paper (optional)

❋ Pencil (optional)

❋ Pins

❋ Ruler

❋ Water-soluble fabric marker or chalk pencil

❋ Turning tool or the tip of a pair of scissors or knitting needle

❋ Small gauge string or crochet cotton

Note: The bodice of this dress has a loose fit, so it will slip on over the head. The skirt length measurements are generous. Adjust the skirt length as needed, depending on where you want the hem to fall.

Cutting

Cut out (or trace with tracing paper and pencil) the Bodice Front and Bodice Back pattern pieces that are provided in the front pocket of this book, in the size you want to make.

FROM THE DRESS FABRIC:

FOR THE SKIRT:

SIZE	XS	S	M	L	XL
Cut 2 Rectangles (L by W)	18 by 34 in/ 46 by 86.5 cm	21 by 37 in/ 53 by 94 cm	24 by 40 in/ 61 by 102 cm	26¾ by 42 in/ 68 by 107 cm	29½ by 44 in/ 75 by 112 cm

After cutting the rectangles, fold each one in half, aligning the shorter edges. At the fold, using scissors clip a notch about ¼ in/6 mm long. These notches will help align the center Front and Back of the Bodice to the skirt.

Cut 1 Bodice Front, *on the fold.*

Cut 1 Bodice Back, *on the fold.*

All sizes: After cutting out the Bodice pieces, using scissors, clip a notch at the fold on the lower edge only, about ¼ in/6 mm long.

For sizes L and XL only: Using a fabric marker or chalk pencil and a ruler, transfer the dart markings from the Bodice Front pattern to the fabric.

FROM THE SASH FABRIC:

FOR THE SASH SIDES:

SIZE	XS AND S	M	L AND XL
Cut 2 Rectangles (L by W)	6½ by 33 in/ 16.5 by 84 cm	8½ by 35 in/ 21.5 by 89 cm	8½ by 37 in/ 21.5 by 94 cm

FOR THE SASH CENTER:

SIZE	XS AND S	M, L, AND XL
Cut 1 Rectangle (L by W)	6½ by 15½ in/ 16.5 by 39 cm	8½ by 18½ in/ 21.5 by 47 cm

Cut enough 1-in/2.5-cm-wide bias strips to make 85 in/216 cm of single-fold bias tape *(see page 20).*

Assemble

STEP 1: SASH

A Place 1 Sash Side piece on top of the Sash Center, with **right** sides together and one set of the short ends aligned, pin. Sew them together with a ¼-in/6-mm seam allowance. Place the second Sash Side piece, with **right** sides together, along the opposite short end of Sash Center and sew them together with a ¼-in/6-mm seam allowance. Press both seams open; then fold the entire Sash in half lengthwise, **right** sides together, aligning the raw edges, and press.

B *Create pointed ends:* With ruler and fabric marker or chalk pencil, make a mark 4 in/10 cm from the short end along the long raw edge. Place the ruler at an angle on the end of the Sash, lining up the mark on the raw edge with the end of the folded edge and draw a straight line. Cut along this line. Repeat on other short end of Sash. *(See illustration.)*

C With **right** sides together, sew Sash raw edges with a ¼-in/6-mm seam allowance, pivoting around the corners and leaving a 5-in/12-cm opening along the long raw edge, so you can turn the Sash **right**-side out. Trim off the excess seam allowance at the corners, being careful to not cut your stitching. *(See illustration.)*

D Turn Sash **right**-side out. Using a turning tool or the tip of a pair of scissors or knitting needle, carefully push out the corners and points. Press the piece flat. Press the raw edges under ¼ in/ 6 mm at the 5-in/12-cm opening, lining them up along the folded edges. Topstitch around the entire perimeter of the Sash, ⅛ in/3 mm from the edge, to close the opening and give the edges a crisp, clean look.

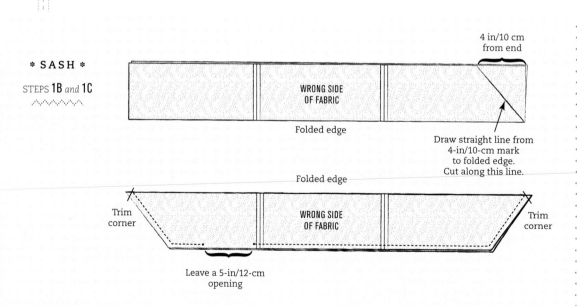

❖ SASH ❖

STEPS **1B** *and* **1C**

WRONG SIDE OF FABRIC

Folded edge

4 in/10 cm from end

Draw straight line from 4-in/10-cm mark to folded edge. Cut along this line.

Folded edge

Trim corner

WRONG SIDE OF FABRIC

Trim corner

Leave a 5-in/12-cm opening

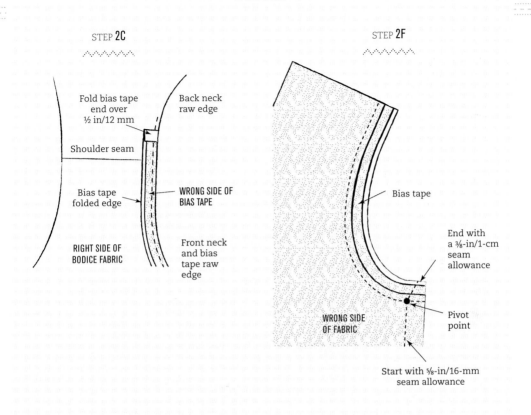

STEP **2C**

Fold bias tape end over ½ in/12 mm

Back neck raw edge

Shoulder seam

Bias tape folded edge

WRONG SIDE OF BIAS TAPE

RIGHT SIDE OF BODICE FABRIC

Front neck and bias tape raw edge

STEP **2F**

Bias tape

End with a ⅜-in/1-cm seam allowance

Pivot point

WRONG SIDE OF FABRIC

Start with ⅝-in/16-mm seam allowance

STEP 2: BODICE

A *For sizes L and XL only:* With **right** sides together, fold darts in half, making sure to line up the markings. Sew along marked lines and tie off the thread ends at the dart point. Press dart seam allowance toward the center Front.

B *For all sizes:* With **right** sides together, align the shoulder raw edges of the Bodice Front and Back pieces, then pin together. Sew each shoulder with a ⅝-in/16-mm seam allowance. Press each seam open. Finish the raw edges in your preferred method *(see page 23)*.

C *Neck edging:* With **right** sides together, beginning and ending along Back neck, leaving approximately 1 in/2.5 cm extra on each end, place bias tape around the neck opening. Unfold one side of the single-fold bias tape, so that the raw edges of the bias tape and the neck opening are aligned, then pin the bias tape around the neck opening. Before sewing the bias tape to the neck opening, with **wrong** sides together, fold one end of the bias tape over ½ in/12 mm. *(See illustration.)* Pin the folded edge into place. Sew the bias tape around the entire neck opening, with a ¼-in/6-mm seam allowance; when you reach the folded end, overlap the bias tape ends ¾ in/2 cm, and trim off any extra bias tape. Clip the seam allowance around the curve, being careful to not cut the stitching.

D   Fold the bias tape to the **wrong** side, enclosing all raw edges. Press the bias tape flat along the inside edge of the neckline, so that it is not visible from the **right** side of the Bodice. With **wrong** side of Bodice and **right** side of bias tape facing up, edge stitch around the outer folded edge of the bias tape.

E   *Armhole finishing:* Follow step 2C, omitting the folded end and overlapping the ends; instead, clip ends of the bias tape to line up with the side seam edges. Fold bias tape to the **wrong** side and press flat as for step 2D, but do not stitch it in place.

F   *Side seams:* Unfold bias tape from **wrong** side of Bodice before stitching side seams. With **right** sides together, line up the Front and Back side seam raw edges and ends of bias tape; pin together. Beginning at the lower edge of the Bodice, sew side seams with a ⅝-in/16-mm seam allowance, stopping at bias tape seam. At the seam, pivot and continue to sew at a slight angle, narrowing the seam allowance to ⅜ in/1 cm at the outer edge of the bias tape. The angle in the seam will allow the bias tape to fold to the **wrong** side easily. *(See illustration on page 39.)*

G   For both armholes, follow step 2D to fold bias tape to **wrong** side and stitch in place.

H   *Sash loops:* From the remainder of the bias tape, cut a piece 12½ in/32 cm long for sizes XS and S, or a piece 15½ in/39 cm long for sizes M, L, and XL. Fold the tape in half lengthwise, enclosing the raw edges, and press. Pin the folded edges together and edge stitch closed. Cut the piece in half, making 2 pieces. Fold these pieces in half to form 2 Loops; align the raw edges of the Loops with the lower edge of the Bodice at each side seam. Baste them in place, ½ in/12 mm from the lower edge.

STEP 3: ASSEMBLE SKIRT/ATTACH TO BODICE

A   Lay both Skirt panels flat, **right** sides together, aligning all raw edges; pin together along both short ends. Sew each side seam together, with a ⅝-in/16-mm seam allowance. Press seams open and finish the raw edges in your preferred method.

B   With the Skirt inside out, use Gathering Method Two *(see page 24)* to gather the upper edge of the Skirt. Place the Bodice inside Skirt with **right** sides together, aligning the raw edges. Match up the Bodice and Skirt pieces at side seams and at center Front and Back notches. Distribute gathers evenly and pin pieces together.

C   Sew the Bodice and Skirt together with a ⅝-in/16-mm seam allowance. Finish the raw edge in your preferred method and press the seam allowance toward the Bodice. Fold the Bodice inside the

Skirt, so that just the seam allowance is sticking out. Place elastic along the back of the Skirt and Bodice seam allowance, baste elastic ends at each side seam, and pin the center of the elastic at center Back. While stretching the elastic, sew onto the Back Skirt seam allowance, directly above the Skirt/Bodice seam. *(See illustration.)*

D *Hem lower edge of Skirt:* With the Dress inside out, fold the raw edge up ¾ in/2 cm and press. Then fold up ¾ in/2 cm and press again. Pin hem in place as needed. Edge stitch along the inner folded edge.

E Turn Dress **right**-side out and remove any visible basting stitches at the waist seam. Give the Dress a good pressing and you're finished! Celebrate with a tea party or picnic.

✵ ASSEMBLE SKIRT/ATTACH TO BODICE ✵

STEP **3C**

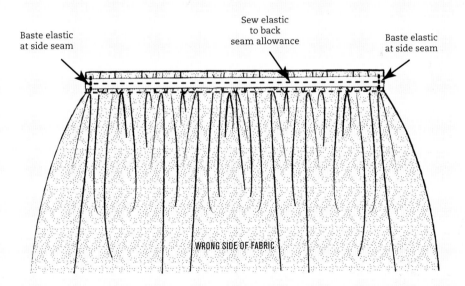

Baste elastic at side seam

Sew elastic to back seam allowance

Baste elastic at side seam

WRONG SIDE OF FABRIC

Tallulah Halter Dress

This fun dress is a breeze to make. It's perfect for a day at
the beach. Just slip it on, tie at the neck, and you're ready to go!
The halter stays in place with comfy elastic at the back,
and the side vents at lower edge of the skirt make it easy
to run, jump, and play. I chose fresh, cheerful colors for
the fabrics to give it that relaxed resort look.

FINISHED SIZE OF DRESS ❋ XS, S, M, L, AND XL

Materials

1 Printed mid-weight cotton fabric (45 in/114 cm wide) for dress and coordinating fabric for lining:

SIZE	XS	S	M	L	XL
Dress	1 yd/ 1 m	1⅛ yd/ 1.1 m	1⅛ yd/ 1.1 m	1¼ yd/ 1.2 m	1¼ yd/ 1.2 m
Lining	⅜ yd/ 35 cm	⅜ yd/ 35 cm	⅜ yd/ 35 cm	⅜ yd/ 35 cm	⅜ yd/ 35 cm

2 Elastic (1 in/2.5 cm wide):

SIZE	XS	S	M	L	XL
Cut Elastic Length	8½ in/ 21.5 cm	9¾ in/ 25 cm	11 in/ 28 cm	12 in/ 30.5 cm	13 in/ 33 cm

3 Coordinating thread

FROM THE SEWING BASKET:

❋ Scissors (for use with paper and fabric)

❋ Tracing paper (optional)

❋ Pencil (optional)

❋ Water-soluble fabric marker or chalk pencil

❋ Ruler

❋ Pins

❋ Turning tool or the tip of a pair of scissors or knitting needle

❋ Safety pin

Cutting

Cut out (or trace with tracing paper and pencil) the Bodice Front, Neck Tie, and Front Skirt pattern pieces that are provided in the front pocket of this book, in the size you want to make.

FROM THE DRESS FABRIC:

FOR BACK SKIRT:

SIZE	XS	S	M	L	XL
Cut 1 Rectangle (L by W)	20 by 16½ in/ 50 by 42 cm	22½ by 17¾ in/ 57 by 45 cm	25 by 19 in/ 63.5 by 48 cm	27¼ by 20 in/ 69 by 50 cm	29½ by 21 in/ 75 by 53 cm

Fold the Back Skirt in half, with **right** sides together, aligning the shorter edges. Using a fabric marker or chalk pencil, mark and then clip to make notches for the side vents as follows:

For sizes XS, S, and M: Using a ruler, measure up from the lower edge, along the side edge 6 in/15 cm and make a mark with fabric marker or chalk pencil.

For sizes L and XL: Using a ruler, measure up from the lower edge, along the side edge, 7 in/18 cm and make a mark with fabric marker or chalk pencil. At this mark, clip a notch about ½ in/12 mm long through both layers.

Fold the remaining dress fabric in half.

Cut 1 Front Skirt piece, *on the fold*. Transfer, then clip notches for side vents and clip a notch at top folded edge.

Cut 2 Bodice Front pieces and 2 Neck Tie pieces. Transfer, then clip a notch at center Front of Bodice on lower edge.

FROM THE LINING FABRIC:

Fold fabric in half, and line up along the selvage edges.

Cut 2 Bodice Front pieces and 2 Neck Tie pieces. Transfer, then clip a notch at center Front of Bodice on lower edge.

STEP 1: BODICE

A Place 1 Bodice Front piece and 1 Neck Tie piece **right** sides together, aligning the raw edges along the shoulder seam. Make sure the Neck Tie tip is pointing toward the bodice neckline. Pin together and sew with a ¼-in/6-mm seam allowance. Press seam open. Repeat on the other Bodice Front/Neck Tie piece and on the 2 sets of Bodice Front/Neck Tie lining pieces. (See illustration.)

B Lay 1 Bodice Front/Tie piece flat, and place 1 Lining piece on top with **right** sides together. Align all edges and pin along the armhole and neckline edges, all the way to the tip of the Tie. Sew these edges together with a ¼-in/6-mm seam allowance, leaving lower edge open. Cut away excess seam allowance at Tie point and make small clips into the seam allowance every couple of inches, being careful to not cut into the stitching. Turn Bodice/Tie **right**-side out. Gently push out the end of the Tie tip using a turning tool or the tip of a pair of scissors or a knitting needle. Press Bodice piece flat and edge stitch along the armhole and neckline. Repeat this step for the other Bodice Front/Lining pieces.

C With both Bodice Front pieces lying side by side, **right** sides facing up, move the piece on the left over, and on top of, the piece on the right, matching up the center Front notches on both pieces and aligning along the lower edge. Note: Bodice Fronts are overlapped, with the right Front (piece on the left) on top of the left Front (piece on the right) at center Front of Bodice. Pin pieces together and baste along the overlapped edge, ⅜ in/1 cm from the raw edge.

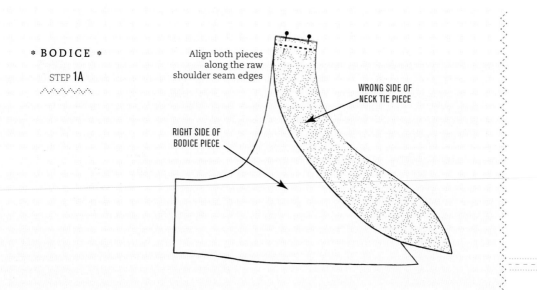

* **BODICE** *

STEP **1A**

Align both pieces along the raw shoulder seam edges

WRONG SIDE OF NECK TIE PIECE

RIGHT SIDE OF BODICE PIECE

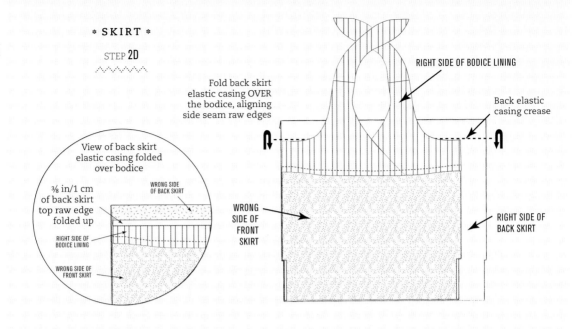

Fold back skirt
elastic casing OVER
the bodice, aligning
side seam raw edges

RIGHT SIDE OF BODICE LINING

Back elastic
casing crease

View of back skirt
elastic casing folded
over bodice

WRONG SIDE
OF BACK SKIRT

⅜ in/1 cm
of back skirt
top raw edge
folded up

RIGHT SIDE OF
BODICE LINING

WRONG SIDE OF
FRONT SKIRT

WRONG
SIDE OF
FRONT
SKIRT

RIGHT SIDE OF
BACK SKIRT

STEP 2: SKIRT (VENTS, CASING, JOINING TO BODICE) AND FINISHING

A *Side vents:* With **wrong** side of 1 of the Skirt pieces facing up, locate side vent notch. Beginning at lower edge, fold and press the seam allowance ¼ in/6 mm to **wrong** side, from lower edge to notch. Fold and press seam allowance again, ¼ in/6 mm. Repeat for each vent side on both Skirt pieces.

B *Join Bodice Front to Front Skirt:* Place Front Skirt and overlapped Bodice pieces, **right** sides together, matching the center Front notches. Align the raw edges and pin. Sew together with a ⅝-in/16-mm seam allowance. Press seam allowances toward the Skirt piece and finish the raw edges in your preferred method *(see page 23)*.

C *Casing:* Lay Back Skirt **right**-side up, fold over top edge 1½ in/4 cm, **right** sides together, and press. Then fold the raw edge up ⅜ in/1 cm, **wrong** sides together, and press. This will eventually form the casing for the elastic.

D *Join side seams:* Unfold the Back Skirt casing and place the Front piece on top, with **right** sides together. Align along one side seam, since the Back Skirt is wider than the Front. The armhole edge of the Front should be placed at the crease of the Back elastic casing. Fold the Back casing over the Bodice Front (you may need to fold the Front down between the Front and Back piece). Pin side seam together, unfolding top of side vent. Beginning at waist edge, sew side seam together with a ⅝-in/16-mm seam allowance, stopping ¼ in/6 mm below the side vent notch. Repeat for other side seam. *(See illustration.)*

Inside view of side vent

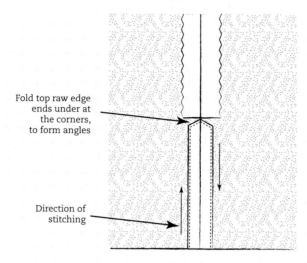

Fold top raw edge
ends under at
the corners,
to form angles

Direction of
stitching

E   *Insert elastic:* Place elastic on the **wrong** side of Back elastic casing, baste elastic to the seam allowance at one side seam. Place a safety pin on the loose end of the elastic. Fold the casing over toward the **wrong** side of the Back Skirt, encasing the elastic. Press and pin casing evenly in place along Back, making sure the elastic is bumped up against the top edge of the fold. Beginning at the side seam that has the elastic basted in place, edge stitch casing to Back Skirt, being careful to not catch elastic in the edge stitching and leaving about a 3-in/7.5-cm opening along the casing seam at the opposite side seam. Using the attached safety pin, work loose end of elastic through casing opening and sew elastic to the seam allowance at the side seam. Edge stitch the opening closed.

F   Clip Front side seam allowance at casing seam and press side seam open. Finish the side seam raw edges in your preferred method.

G   *Finish vents:* With Dress inside out, fold the top raw edge ends of the side vents under at the corners to form a slight angle, and press. Starting at the lower edge of side vent, edge stitch the inner folded edge in place. Pivot around top of slit and continue edge stitching down other side of vent. *(See illustration.)*

H   *Hem:* With the Dress inside out, fold the lower edge up ¾ in/2 cm and press. Then fold ¾ in/ 2 cm and press again; pin hem in place as needed. Edge stitch along the inner folded edge.

I   Turn Dress **right**-side out and give a final pressing. You're done! Perfect for a backyard pool party or stroll along the beach.

· № 3 ·

Josie Dress

This dress was originally designed for an eighth-grade
graduation. Since then it's become a hit with my Sis Boom
customers. Mix up the fabrics to make a more whimsical
dress or use just one fabric for a sophisticated look.
For a very special occasion, just add a crinoline
and attach a ruffle to the bottom. Fancy!

FINISHED SIZE OF DRESS ✴ XS, S, M, L, AND XL

Materials

1 Printed mid-weight cotton fabric (45 in/114 cm wide) for dress and coordinating fabric for lining:

SIZE	XS	S	M	L	XL
Bodice, Bodice Lining, and Straps	½ yd/ 45 cm	½ yd/ 45 cm	¾ yd/ 70 cm	¾ yd/ 70 cm	¾ yd/ 70 cm
SHORT Skirt	1 yd/ 1 m	1¼ yd/ 1.2 m	1⅜ yd/ 1.3 m	1⅝ yd/ 1.5 m	1¾ yd/ 1.6 m
LONG Skirt	(See note.)	1½ yd/ 1.4 m	2 yd/ 2 m	2¼ yd/ 2.2 m	2⅜ yd/ 2.3 m
Waist Tie	⅜ yd/ 35 cm	⅜ yd/ 35 cm	⅜ yd/ 35 cm	⅜ yd/ 35 cm	⅜ yd/ 35 cm

2 12-in/30.5-cm polyester coil zipper

3 Coordinating thread

FROM THE SEWING BASKET:

❁ Scissors (for use with paper and fabric)

❁ Tracing paper (optional)

❁ Pencil (optional)

❁ Water-soluble fabric marker or chalk pencil

❁ Ruler

❁ Pins

❁ Turning tool or the tip of a pair of scissors or knitting needle

❁ Small gauge string or crochet cotton

❁ Zipper foot for sewing machine

❁ Seam ripper

Note: The bodice of this dress has a snug fit, so there is a back zipper for ease in dressing. Both the long and short skirt length measurements are generous. Adjust the skirt length as needed, depending on where you want the hem of this dress to fall. There are no long skirt length measurements given for the XS size since a full-length dress might be a bit impractical for a toddler.

Cut out (or trace with tracing paper and pencil) the Bodice Front, Waist Front, Bodice Lining, and Bodice Back pattern pieces that are provided in the front pocket of this book, in the size you want to make.

FROM THE SKIRT FABRIC, FOR SHORT DRESS LENGTH:

FOR THE BACK SKIRT:

SIZE	XS	S	M	L	XL
Cut 2 Rectangles (L by W)	18 by 15½ in/ 46 by 39 cm	21 by 16¾ in/ 53 by 42.5 cm	24 by 18 in/ 61 by 46 cm	26¾ by 19¼ in/ 68 by 49 cm	29½ by 21 in/ 75 by 53 cm

FOR THE FRONT SKIRT:

SIZE	XS	S	M	L	XL
Cut 1 Rectangle (L by W)	18 by 30 in/ 46 by 76 cm	21 by 32½ in/ 53 by 82.5 cm	24 by 35 in/ 61 by 89 cm	26¾ by 37½ in/ 68 by 95 cm	29½ by 41 in/ 75 by 104 cm

FROM THE SKIRT FABRIC, FOR LONG DRESS LENGTH:

Since our sizes cover many different heights within each range, the best way to get an accurate long dress length is to measure the wearer from the waist (about where her belly button is), down to the ankle or floor. If you plan to make a floor-length dress, remember to have the recipient put on the actual shoes she will be wearing with the dress before you measure her. Once you have your measurement, add 2 in/5 cm to that measurement for seam and hem allowances. For example, if the waist-to-floor measurement is 35 in/89 cm, add 2 in/5 cm for a total cut length of 37 in/94 cm. Jot down the needed cut length on a separate sheet.

FOR THE BACK SKIRT:

SIZE	S	M	L	XL
Cut 2 Rectangles (L by W)	L by 16¾ in/ L by 42.5 cm	L by 18 in/ L by 46 cm	L by 19¼ in/ L by 49 cm	L by 21 in/ L by 53 cm

FOR THE FRONT SKIRT:

SIZE	S	M	L	XL
Cut 1 Rectangle (L by W)	L by 32½ in/ L by 82.5 cm	L by 35 in/ L by 89 cm	L by 37½ in/ L by 95 cm	L by 41 in/ L by 104 cm

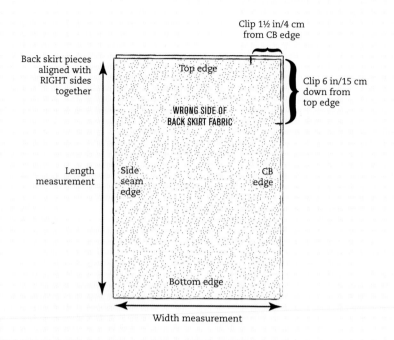

Clip 1½ in/4 cm
from CB edge

Back skirt pieces
aligned with
RIGHT sides
together

Top edge

Clip 6 in/15 cm
down from
top edge

WRONG SIDE OF
BACK SKIRT FABRIC

Length
measurement

Side
seam
edge

CB
edge

Bottom edge

Width measurement

After cutting out the Skirt pieces (short or long length), mark and notch them: Fold the Front Skirt piece in half lengthwise. At one end of the fold, clip a notch about ¼ in/6 mm long; this is the center Front waist edge of the Skirt. Lay both Back Skirt pieces one on top of the other, **right** sides together, aligning all the raw edges. Along one of the length measurement sides, with a fabric marker or chalk pencil, make a mark 6 in/15 cm down from the upper edge. Clip a ¼-in/6-mm notch at this mark for the zipper notch, through both layers. This will now be referred to as the center Back seam. On the upper edge, using a ruler, measure out from the center Back seam 1½ in/4 cm and make a mark. Clip a ¼-in/6-mm notch at this mark through both layers; this will now be referred as the Back waist edge. (See illustration.)

FROM BODICE FABRIC:
Fold fabric in half, lining up selvage edges.

Cut 1 Bodice Front piece, on the fold. After cutting out the Bodice Front piece, clip a notch ¼ in/6 mm long, at the top and lower edge of the fold and at the indicated notches for the gathering.

Cut 1 Bodice Lining piece, on the fold. Clip a ¼-in/6-mm long notch at the upper and lower edges of the fold.

Cut 4 Bodice Back pieces. You want 2 mirror image sets, 1 for the outside of the Dress and 1 for the Lining. Clip a ¼-in-/6-mm-long notch at the Bodice Back upper edge, where indicated on ¼-in-/6-mm-long pattern.

SIZE	XS	S	M	L	XL
Cut 2 Rectangles (L by W)	8¼ by 2 in/ 21 by 5 cm	9 by 2 in/ 23 by 5 cm	9¾ by 2 in/ 25 by 5 cm	10½ by 2 in/ 26.5 by 5 cm	11¼ by 2 in/ 28.5 by 5 cm

FROM THE WAIST TIE FABRIC:

FOR THE WAIST TIES:

SIZE	XS	S	M	L	XL
Cut 2 Rectangles (L by W)	4½ by 27 in/ 11 by 68.5 cm	4½ by 29 in/ 11 by 74 cm	5 by 31 in/ 12 by 79 cm	5¼ by 33 in/ 13 by 84 cm	5¼ by 35 in/ 13 by 89 cm

Cut 1 Waist Front piece, *on the fold*. After cutting out the Waist Front piece, clip a notch ¼ in/6 mm long, at the upper and lower edges of the fold, and at the notches indicating gathering placement.

STEP 1: STRAPS AND WAIST TIES

A   *Straps:* Fold Strap piece in half lengthwise, with **right** sides together, pin, and press. Sew the long raw edges together, with ¼-in/6-mm seam allowance. Turn **right**-side out and press flat, with the seam along one edge. This edge will be referred to as the *seamed edge* and opposite edge will be referred to as the *folded edge* of the Straps. Repeat for other Strap.

B   *Waist Ties:* Fold 1 Waist Tie in half lengthwise, with **right** sides together; align the raw edges and press. With a ruler and fabric marker or chalk pencil, make a mark 2½ in/6 cm from one end, along the long raw edge. Place the ruler at an angle on the end of the Waist Tie, line up the mark with the end of the folded edge, and draw a straight line. Cut along this line. *(See illustration on page 56.)*

C   With **right** sides together, starting at the pointed end and continuing along the long raw edge sew Waist Tie raw edges with a ¼-in/6-mm seam allowance, leaving the straight short end open. Trim off the excess seam allowance at the corner and point, being careful to not cut stitching.

D   Turn Waist Tie **right**-side out. Carefully push out the corner and point using a turning tool or the tip of a pair of scissors or knitting needle. Press Tie flat.

E   Repeat steps B through D on the other Waist Tie.

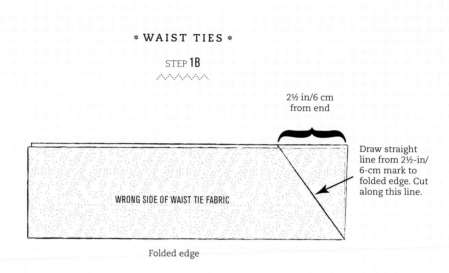

✳ WAIST TIES ✳

STEP 1B

2½ in/6 cm
from end

Draw straight
line from 2½-in/
6-cm mark to
folded edge. Cut
along this line.

WRONG SIDE OF WAIST TIE FABRIC

Folded edge

STEP 2: BODICE

A   On Bodice Front piece, use Gathering Method One (*see page* 24) to add gathers between the notches at the neckline and waist seam. With **right** sides together, align the lower edge of the Bodice Front piece with the upper edge of the Waist Front piece. Pin together and distribute the gathers evenly between the notches. Sew together with a ⅝-in/16-mm seam allowance. Clip the seam allowance at the curves, being careful not to cut the stitching. Press seam allowance toward Waist Front piece.

B   *Waist Ties:* Lay Bodice Front/Waist Front piece **right**-side up; line up 1 Waist Tie piece at side edge of Waist Front, making sure that the Waist Tie folded edge is aligned with the Bodice/Waist Front seam. Pin together and baste Waist Tie in place ⅜ in/1 cm from the edge. Repeat with other Waist Tie on the opposite side edge.

C   *Side seams:* Place 1 Bodice Back piece on top of Bodice Front, **right** sides together, and align along side edge; pin in place. Sew side seam together with ⅝-in/16-mm seam allowance. Press seam open. Repeat for the opposite side seam.

D   *Lining side seams:* With **right** sides together, align the Bodice Front Lining with 1 Bodice Back Lining piece, along side edges. Pin and sew together with a ⅝-in/16-mm seam allowance. Press seam open. Repeat for the opposite side seam.

❈ BODICE ❈

STEP 2E

〜〜〜〜〜

Center strap along
top bodice raw edge

Baste strap
ends in place

Line up folded edge
of strap with notch
at back bodice edge

Seamed edge
of strap

Close-up of strap
centered along top bodice
edge. Place about ⅜ in/
1 cm from each edge

⅜ in/1 cm

RIGHT SIDE
OF BODICE

Folded edge
of strap

E   *Attach Straps:* With **right** side of Bodice *facing up* and folded edge of Strap facing toward center Front, center end of Strap along upper Bodice straight edge (there will be about ⅜ in/1 cm of Bodice visible on each side of Strap). Pin in place. Baste Strap to Bodice Front, ¼ in/6 mm from upper edge. Place the other strap end with the folded edge of strap at the Bodice Back notch, aligning raw edges of Strap and upper edge of Back. Pin in place (the Strap should have a slight half twist to it). Baste Strap to Back, ¼ in/6 mm from upper edge. Repeat on opposite side with other strap. *(See illustration.)*

F   With Lining piece lying flat, **right** side facing up, place Bodice piece on top, **right** sides together. Align along upper raw edges, distributing the Front neckline gathers evenly, and pin together. Sew along top edges with a ⅜-in/1-cm seam allowance, pivoting where necessary at the Front Strap and being careful to only sew the Straps into this seam where they are basted in place. You don't want to catch the Strap in the armhole seam. Trim off seam allowance at corners beside Straps and make small clips in the seam allowance at armhole and neckline curves, being careful not to clip the stitching.

❋ BODICE ❋

STEP **2G**
〰〰〰〰

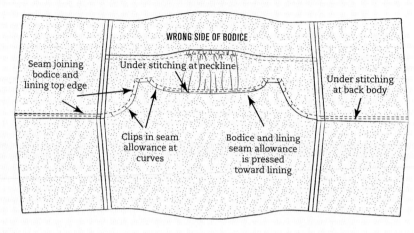

After stitching bodice and lining
together along the top edge,
unfold the two pieces so they
are facing WRONG side up

WRONG SIDE OF BODICE

Seam joining
bodice and
lining top edge

Under stitching at neckline

Under stitching
at back body

Clips in seam
allowance at
curves

Bodice and lining
seam allowance
is pressed
toward lining

G Unfold the Bodice and Lining, so they form a single layer with **wrong** side facing up. You will not be able to get this perfectly flat, but do the best you can. With the neck edge seam as flat as possible, press the seam allowance toward the lining. Under stitch *(see page 28)* the seam allowance to the lining at the Front neckline gathers and Bodice Back. *(See illustration.)*

H Fold the Bodice and Lining pieces, **wrong** sides together, and press flat along neck, armhole, and back edge. Align the bottom raw edges and baste both layers together ½ in/12 mm from lower edge, to keep layers from shifting.

STEP 3: ASSEMBLE SKIRT/ATTACH TO BODICE

A Lay Skirt Front flat, **right** side facing up. Lay the Skirt Back pieces on top of the Skirt Front, with **right** sides together, aligning along the side edges; be sure the Skirt Back notched edges (waist edges) are facing in the same direction as Skirt Front waist edge, and that the notches for the zipper are pointing toward each other (center Back). Pin both of the side edges and sew together with a ⅝-in/16-mm seam allowance. Press seams open and finish the raw edges in your preferred method *(see page 23)*.

B *Gather Skirt:* Using Gathering Method Two *(see page 24)*, gather the upper edge of the Skirt. Place lined Bodice piece on top of the Skirt with **right** sides together, aligning the raw edges. Match the pieces at side seams, center Front notches, and center Back edges. Distribute gathers evenly and pin.

C Beginning at center Back, sew the lined Bodice and Skirt together using a ⅝-in/16-mm seam allowance. Finish the raw edge in your preferred method and press the seam allowance toward the Bodice.

D *Back seam:* With **right** sides together, align the center Back edges of Dress and pin. Beginning at the lower edge of the Skirt, sew seam with a ⅝-in/16-mm seam allowance, stopping at notches for the zipper; backstitch. Lengthen the stitch length on the sewing machine to baste and baste the rest of the center Back seam of Skirt and Bodice closed. Press seam open and finish raw edges in your preferred method.

E *Hem:* With the dress inside out, fold edge up ¾ in/2 cm and press. Then fold ¾ in/2 cm and press again, pinning as needed. Edge stitch along the inner folded edge.

F Turn dress **right**-side out. Measure 5½ in/14 cm down from waist seam at center Back and mark with a pin. With a fabric marker or chalk pencil and ruler, draw a straight line down each side of center Back seam (Bodice and Skirt), ¼ in/6 mm from seam; end at the pin.

G Turn Dress inside out. Put the zipper foot on your sewing machine. Lay the zipper **right**-side down along inside center Back seam allowance, so the zipper teeth are centered along the basted seam and the zipper head is about ⅛ in/3 mm down from the Back neck edge of Dress. Pin the zipper in place, pinning *only* through the zipper tape and seam allowance, *not* through the Dress. Fold back the outside layer; baste the zipper to each side of the center Back seam allowance. The basting stitches will not be visible from the **right** side of the Dress. *(See illustration.)*

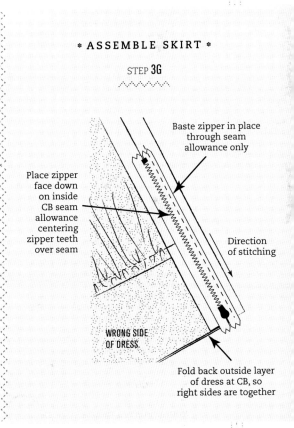

❋ ASSEMBLE SKIRT ❋

STEP **3G**

Baste zipper in place through seam allowance only

Place zipper face down on inside CB seam allowance centering zipper teeth over seam

Direction of stitching

WRONG SIDE OF DRESS.

Fold back outside layer of dress at CB, so right sides are together

H   Turn the Dress **right**-side out. Tuck the top ends of the zipper tape under, so they're between the body of the Dress and seam allowance. Pin the zipper tape ends in place. Along each of the drawn lines at center Back, sew from the bottom of the zipper to the Back neck edge, stitching through all layers. Once both sides of the zipper are stitched down, go back and stitch along the lower edge to connect the vertical stitch lines. *(See illustration.)* Use a seam ripper to carefully remove the basting stitches that are keeping the center Back seam closed. On the smaller sizes, trim off the excess length of zipper on the inside, leaving about 1 in/2.5 cm below the lower edge of the horizontal stitching. Zigzag the end of cut zipper, so it doesn't come apart. All finished! Now, how about a fancy garden party?

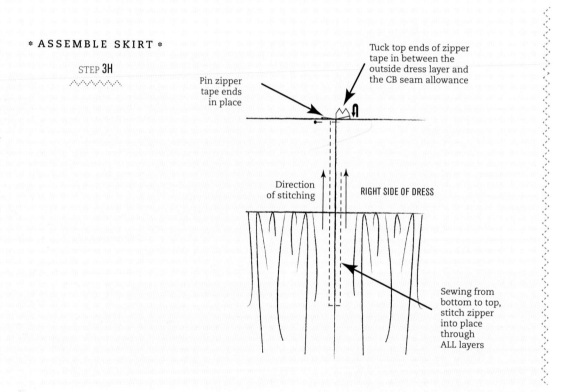

❄ ASSEMBLE SKIRT ❄

STEP **3H**

Pin zipper tape ends in place

Tuck top ends of zipper tape in between the outside dress layer and the CB seam allowance

Direction of stitching

RIGHT SIDE OF DRESS

Sewing from bottom to top, stitch zipper into place through ALL layers

· № 4 ·

Agnes Tunic Dress

Here's a dress that's sweet and stylish at the same time, the combination of the different fabrics makes a playful statement. Throw it on over a pair of leggings or wear alone. Either way it's totally comfortable and easy to wear all year round. We love our Agnes tunic!

FINISHED SIZE OF DRESS ❋ XS, S, M, L, AND XL

Materials

1 Printed mid-weight cotton (45 in/114 cm wide) fabric for Dress and a coordinating fabric for the Neck band, Sleeve bands, and Hem band:

SIZE	XS	S	M	L	XL
Dress	1 yd/ 1 m	1⅛ yd/ 1.1 m	1½ yd/ 1.4 m	1¾ yd/ 1.6 m	1⅞ yd/ 1.8 m
Coordinating Fabric	½ yd/ 45 cm	½ yd/ 45 cm	⅞ yd/ 80 cm	⅞ yd/ 80 cm	⅞ yd/ 80 cm

2 Lightweight fusible interfacing:

SIZE	XS	S	M	L	XL
Interfacing	¼ yd/ 23 cm	¼ yd/ 23 cm	¼ yd/ 23 cm	¼ yd/ 23 cm	¼ yd/ 23 cm

3 1 button (½ in/12 mm diameter)

4 Coordinating thread

FROM THE SEWING BASKET:

❋ Scissors (for use with paper and fabric)
❋ Tracing paper (optional)
❋ Pencil (optional)
❋ Water-soluble fabric marker or chalk pencil
❋ Ruler
❋ Pins
❋ Seam ripper
❋ Hand-sewing needle

Cutting

Cut out (or trace with tracing paper and pencil) the Front, Back, Sleeve, Front Neck, and Back Neck pattern pieces that are provided in the front pocket of this book, in the size you want to make.

FROM THE DRESS FABRIC:

Cut 1 Front piece, *on the fold*. After cutting out the Front piece, clip a ¼-in/6-mm notch at the upper edge of the fold, and where indicated on pattern for gathering. With a fabric marker, or chalk pencil, and ruler mark the ⅜-in/1-cm seam allowance on the **wrong** side of fabric at Front neck. Clip into the corners of the seam allowance about ¼ in/6 mm. *(See illustration.)*

Cut 1 Back piece, *on the fold*. After cutting out the Back piece, cut a 3-in-/7.5-cm-long slit from the neck edge along the center Back fold, for the Keyhole neck opening.

Cut 2 Sleeve pieces, *on the fold*.

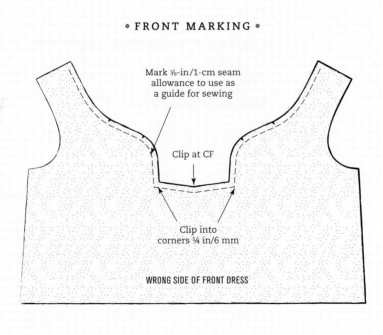

❊ FRONT MARKING ❊

Mark ⅜-in/1-cm seam allowance to use as a guide for sewing

Clip at CF

Clip into corners ¼ in/6 mm

WRONG SIDE OF FRONT DRESS

FROM THE COORDINATING FABRIC:

FOR THE SLEEVE BANDS:

SIZE	XS	S	M	L	XL
Cut 2 Rectangles (L by W)	13 by 4¾ in/ 33 by 12 cm	14½ by 4¾ in/ 37 by 12 cm	15¾ by 5¾ in/ 40 by 14.5 cm	17 by 5¾ in/ 43 by 14.5 cm	18¼ by 5¾ in/ 46 by 14.5 cm

FOR THE HEM BAND:

SIZE	XS	S	M	L	XL
Cut 1 Rectangle (L by W)	6¼ by 36½ in/ 16 by 93 cm	6¼ by 40¾ in/ 16 by 103.5 cm			
Cut 2 Rectangles (L by W)			7¼ by 23¼ in/ 18.5 by 59 cm	7¼ by 25¼ in/ 18.5 by 64 cm	7¼ by 27¼ in/ 18.5 by 69 cm

Cut 2 Front Neck pieces *on the fold*, and 4 Back Neck pieces. To make sure you have enough fabric to cut the Front Neck pieces on the fold, fold fabric in half, align both selvage edges, and crease down center. Unfold; then fold each selvage in toward the center crease, **right** sides together. The 4 Back Neck pieces don't need to be cut on the fold, but you do want to make sure you have 2 mirror-image sets of the Back Neck pieces.

Cut 1 bias strip measuring 12 in/30.5 cm by 1 in/2.5 cm. After cutting bias strip, follow the instructions on page 20 to make bias strip into double-fold binding. You should end up with a piece of bias tape that is ¼ in/6 mm wide and 12 in/30.5 cm long.

FROM THE INTERFACING FABRIC:

Cut 1 Front Neck piece, *on the fold*.

Cut 2 Back Neck pieces.

Assemble

STEP 1: NECKLINE PIECES

A *Interfacing:* Lay one pair of Back Neck pieces and one Front Neck piece on a flat surface, **wrong** side facing up; align interfacing pieces on top, with fusible-side down. Fuse with an iron, according to manufacturer's instructions. These fused pieces will be the **right** side Neck pieces.

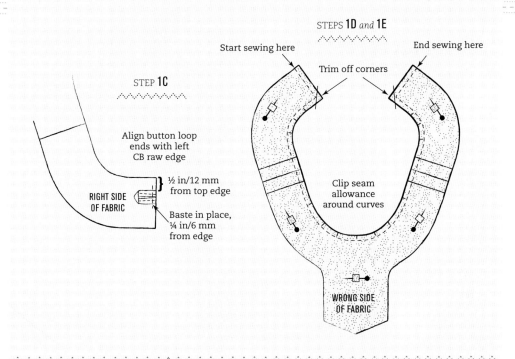

B   Align and pin the **right** side Neck pieces (pieces with the interfacing) at the shoulder edges. Sew each shoulder seam together with a ⅝-in/16-mm seam allowance. Press seams open. Repeat for the remaining Front and Back Neck pieces (without interfacing) for Neck lining.

C   *Button Loop:* Cut off 2 in/5 cm from the piece of bias tape and edge stitch closed along the long edge of tape. Fold the Button Loop in half, and align the ends with left center Back raw edge of interfaced Neck piece, ½ in/12 mm down from neck raw edge. Pin and baste in place, ¼ in/6 mm from center Back edge. *(See illustration.)*

D   *Attach Neck Piece Lining:* Lay the interfaced Neck Piece flat with **right** side facing up. Align and pin the Neck Piece Lining piece on top, with **right** sides together. Sew together with a ⅜-in/1-cm seam allowance, starting from the lower edge of center Back, around the inner neckline and ending at the other center Back edge, pivoting at corners. *(See illustration.)*

E   Trim off center Back neck corners and make small clips into the seam allowance around the neckline curve, being careful to not cut the stitching. Turn Neck Piece **right**-side out and press. *(See illustration.)*

F   Align Neck Piece layers along lower raw edge, and pin the layers together, so they don't shift. Baste the layers together ¼ in/6 mm from raw edge. Set Neckline Piece aside.

STEP 2: BODY

A *Apply bias tape to Back Keyhole:* With **wrong** side facing up, unfold bias tape and align raw edge of tape along raw edge of Keyhole. *Note:* It's helpful, when you are applying the bias tape to the Keyhole, to have the Keyhole raw edges folded out so that they form a continuous straight line, instead of trying to sew around the tight curve at the bottom. Sew the bias tape to the Keyhole, along the first crease in the bias tape from the raw edge, about ¼ in/6 mm from the edge. Trim the seam allowance down to ⅛ in/3 mm. Wrap the bias tape around the seam allowance to the **right** side of the Back, enclosing the raw edges. Fold raw edge of bias tape under, along crease, and edge stitch bias tape to Keyhole on **right** side of garment, making sure to cover the stitching that shows from the **wrong** side. Cut away the excess length of bias tape. Turn piece to **wrong** side; fold Back in half and align Keyhole edges. Sew a small diagonal seam at the bottom of the Keyhole; this will keep the bottom of the Keyhole in place, so it doesn't flip to the outside. *(See illustration.)*

B *Gather Front Neck:* On Front, sew basting stitches, using Gathering Method One *(see page 24)*, where gathering is indicated at Front neckline.

C *Join Shoulders:* With **right** sides together, align Front and Back pieces at the shoulder edges and pin together. Sew each shoulder seam with a ⅝-in/16-mm seam allowance. Press seams open and finish the raw edges in your preferred method *(see page 23)*.

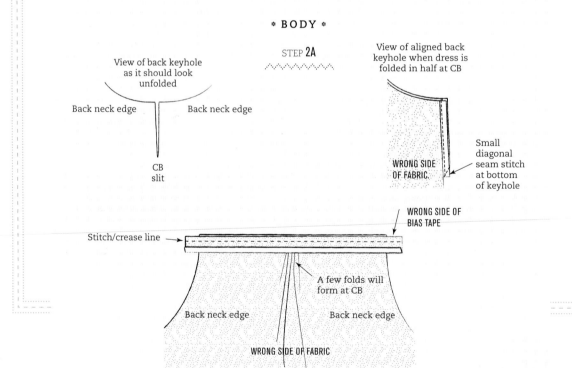

❊ BODY ❊

STEP **2A**

View of back keyhole as it should look unfolded

Back neck edge   Back neck edge

CB slit

View of aligned back keyhole when dress is folded in half at CB

WRONG SIDE OF FABRIC.

Small diagonal seam stitch at bottom of keyhole

WRONG SIDE OF BIAS TAPE

Stitch/crease line →

A few folds will form at CB

Back neck edge   Back neck edge

WRONG SIDE OF FABRIC

D *Attach Neckline Piece:* Lay the joined Front and Back piece (Body) flat, **right** side facing up; lay Neckline Piece on top, with **right** sides together, and align raw edges. Pin raw edges together, making sure both pieces are lined up at the center Back, shoulder seams, gathering notches, and center Front. Distribute the gathers evenly as you pin. Take your time with this step, and use as many pins as you need, since there are some curves and angles to sew around. With the **wrong** side of the Body facing up, slowly sew the Body and Neck pieces together using a ⅜-in/1-cm seam allowance, making sure to follow the marked seam allowance at the lower edge of Neck. Make small clips into seam allowance around the entire neckline, being careful to not cut the stitching. Remove any visible basting stitches with a seam ripper. Zigzag the raw edges and press seam allowance toward the Body.

E *Sleeves:* With Body lying flat, pin the Sleeves into each armhole, with **right** sides together. Sew together with a ⅝-in/16-mm seam allowance. Press seam allowance toward Sleeve and finish the raw edges in your preferred method.

F With **right** sides together, align and pin raw edges at the side and Sleeve seams. Beginning at the lower edge of the side, sew seam together with a ⅝-in/16-mm seam allowance, finishing at the lower edge of the Sleeve. Press seam open and finish raw edges in your preferred method. Repeat on other side.

STEP 3: FINISHING

A *Sleeve Bands:* Fold Sleeve Band in half, with **right** sides together, matching along the short ends. Sew together with a ⅝-in/16-mm seam allowance, to form a tube. Press seam open. Fold tube in half lengthwise with **wrong** sides together; align along the raw edges and press. Repeat for other Sleeve Band.

B *Hem Band:* Sizes XS and S only: Follow the instructions given for Sleeve Bands (step 3A). Sizes M, L, and XL only: Align both Hem Band pieces, with **right** sides together, along all edges. Sew each short end together with a ⅝-in/16-mm seam allowance, to form a tube. Press both seams open. Fold tube in half lengthwise with **wrong** sides together; align along the raw edges and press.

C *Attach Sleeve Bands:* With Dress **right**-side out, slip a Sleeve Band over the lower edge of the Sleeve, aligning the raw edges and matching the Sleeve Band seam with the underarm seam; pin. Sew together with a ⅝-in/16-mm seam allowance. Press seam allowance toward Sleeve and finish the raw edges in your preferred method. Repeat for other Sleeve.

D *Attach Hem Band:* With Dress **right**-side out, slip the Hem band over the lower edge of the Dress, aligning the raw edges and matching the side seam(s) with the Hem Band seam(s); pin. Sew together with a ⅝-in/16-mm seam allowance. Press seam allowance toward body and finish the raw edges in your preferred method.

E *Button:* Align center Back neck edges; with a fabric marker, make a mark on the right Back neck, inside the Button Loop overlap. Using needle and thread, sew button on top of mark.

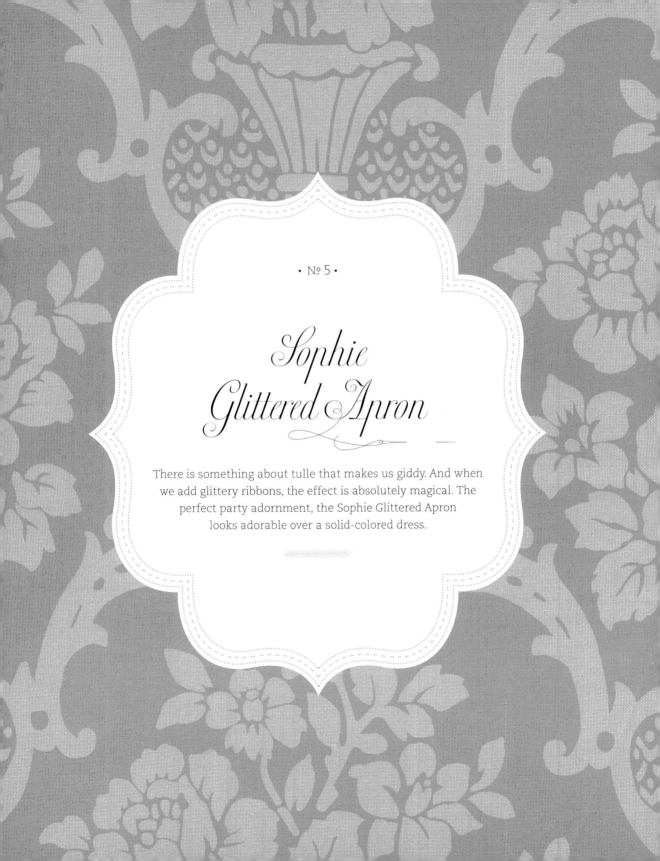

Sophie Glittered Apron

There is something about tulle that makes us giddy. And when we add glittery ribbons, the effect is absolutely magical. The perfect party adornment, the Sophie Glittered Apron looks adorable over a solid-colored dress.

FINISHED SIZE OF APRON (not including ties)

❋ **XS AND S:** 17 in/43 cm length by 30 in/76 cm width at lower edge

❋ **M, L, AND XL:** 21 in/53 cm length by 36 in/91 cm width at lower edge

Materials

1 Nylon tulle (54 in/137 cm wide) for Apron:

SIZE	XS AND S	M, L, AND XL
Tulle Fabric	⅞ yd/ 80 cm	1 yd/ 91 cm

2 Glitter ribbon (⅜ in/1 cm wide) for decoration (see "Resources," page 172):

SIZE	XS AND S	M, L, AND XL
Glitter Ribbon Color A	⅞ yd/ 80 cm	1 yd/ 91 cm
Glitter Ribbon Color B	⅞ yd/ 80 cm	1 yd/ 91 cm
Glitter Ribbon Color C	⅞ yd/ 80 cm	1 yd/ 91 cm

3 Glitter ribbon (1½ in/4 cm wide) for Waist Tie (see "Resources," page 172):

SIZE	XS AND S	M, L, AND XL
Glitter Ribbon Color A	1¼ yd/ 1.2 m	1½ yd/ 1.4 m

4 Coordinating thread

FROM THE SEWING BASKET:

❋ Scissors (for use with fabric)

❋ Ruler

❋ Pins

❋ Water-soluble fabric marker or chalk pencil

Cutting

FROM TULLE FABRIC FOR APRON:

SIZE	XS AND S	M, L, AND XL
Cut 1 rectangle (L by W)	30 by 32 in/ 76 by 81 cm	36 by 40 in/ 91 by 101 cm

Assemble

A Place Apron piece on a flat surface. Attach decorative Ribbon: Using a ruler, place Ribbon Color B 2 in/5 cm up from one of the shorter edges and pin in place. Edge stitch ribbon to Apron. Place Ribbon Color A ⅜ in/1 cm above Ribbon Color B and pin in place. Edge stitch ribbon to Apron. Repeat for Ribbon Color C, ⅜ in/1 cm above Color A. The side of the fabric with ribbon sewn on is the **right** side of fabric.

B Place the Waist Tie ribbon on a flat surface, with **right** side facing down. From each end, using a ruler, measure in toward center 17 in/43 cm for sizes XS and S and 20½ in/52 cm for sizes M, L, and XL; make a mark at each side with a fabric marker or chalk pencil. *(See illustration.)*

C Fold Apron in half, aligning the shorter edges, with **wrong** sides together (ribbon is facing out). Along the folded edge of fabric, use Gathering Method One *(see page 24)* and run 2 rows of basting stitches ⅜ in/1 cm and ⅝ in/16 mm from the folded edge.

D Gather the Apron fabric and place the **right** side of Apron against the **wrong** side of Waist Tie, between the 2 marks. Overlap the fabric and ribbon ½ in/12 mm, distributing the gathers evenly; pin Apron to Waist Tie. Sew the Apron piece to the Waist Tie, ⅛ in/3 mm from Waist Tie edge. Remove any visible basting threads and clip Waist Tie ends into V shapes. *(See illustration.)*

❋ ASSEMBLE ❋

STEPS **B** and **D**

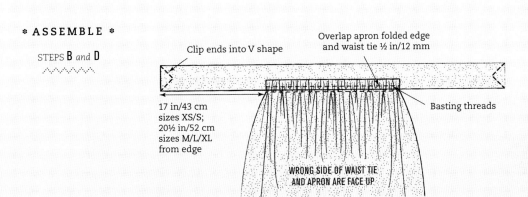

Clip ends into V shape

Overlap apron folded edge and waist tie ½ in/12 mm

Basting threads

17 in/43 cm sizes XS/S; 20½ in/52 cm sizes M/L/XL from edge

WRONG SIDE OF WAIST TIE AND APRON ARE FACE UP

· № 6 ·

Georgia Tulle Ballet Skirt

Whether your little girl dreams of being a dancer or just loves dressing up, hearing the rustling of tulle and petals as she moves is sure to tickle her fancy. You can keep the skirt simple with very few embellishments, or decorate it with lots of flowers, ribbons, and even glitter.

FINISHED SIZE OF SKIRT

✽ **SIZE XS AND S:** 13½ in/34 cm long by 80 in/2.03 m lower edge circumference

✽ **SIZE M, L, AND XL:** 18½ in/47 cm long by 100 in/2.54 m lower edge circumference

Materials

1 Nylon tulle (54 in/137 cm wide) for Skirt:

SIZE	XS AND S	M, L, AND XL
Nylon Tulle Fabric	4½ yd/ 4.25 m	11¼ yd/ 10.3 m

2 Elastic (½ in/12 mm wide) for waist:

SIZE	XS AND S	M, L, AND XL
Elastic	⅝ yd/ 57 cm	¾ yd/ 70 cm

3 Coordinating thread

4 60 to 150 silk flower petals and leaves for Skirt (see "Resources," page 172)

5 Fine glitter (optional)

6 1¼ yd/114 cm ribbon (2 in/5 cm wide) for decoration at waist

FROM THE SEWING BASKET:

✽ Scissors (for use with fabric)

✽ Ruler

✽ Water-soluble fabric marker or chalk pecil

✽ Pins

✽ Safety pin

FROM THE CRAFT CABINET:

✽ White glue (optional)

✽ ½-in/12-mm sponge brush (optional)

✽ Dual-temperature glue gun and glue sticks (optional)

Cutting

It is very helpful to have a large flat area (a clean floor works well) to use when laying out and cutting the tulle. Tulle is usually sold off the bolt, with the fabric width folded in half. Keep it folded in half and lightly press out any wrinkles. This fold will be referred to as the *center crease*.

FROM TULLE FABRIC:

SIZES XS AND S:

Cut the 4½-yd/4.25-m piece in half, to get two 2¼-yd/2.125-m pieces. Unfold 1 piece of the fabric, so that it's a single layer and measures 81 by 54 in/2.06 by 1.22 m. Fold both of the 81-in/206-cm edges in toward the center crease. *(See illustration on page 78.)*

Place the second piece of fabric, still folded in half, on top of the first piece. Align the center creases, and then unfold the top piece so it's flat. Fold *both* edges in toward the center crease, as you did for first piece. You will have 4 layers of tulle.

Now fold both of these pieces in half along the center crease, making sure the raw edges are inside the fold. There are now a total of 8 layers of tulle. Pin all of the layers together, about 1 in/2.5 cm from the center creases.

SIZES M, L, AND XL:

Cut the 11¼-yd/10.3-m piece in half crosswise, to get 2 pieces that are 5⅝ yd/5.14 m long. Then cut each of these pieces in half; you will have 4 pieces that measure about 101 in/2.57 m long. *(See illustration on page 78.)*

Lay each of the 4 pieces on top of one another, aligned along the center crease. You will have 8 layers of tulle. Pin all of the layers together along the folded edges. Measure with a ruler and mark with a fabric marker or chalk pencil 20 in/51 cm from fold along the entire length and draw a straight line across. Pin the layers together close to the line and cut along the line. You will now have a rectangle that measures 101 by 20 in/2.57 m by 51 cm.

Press the long cut edges over ½ in/12 mm. Then fold over 1 in/2.5 cm and press again. Pin folded edge in place as you go. This will be the elastic casing.

FROM THE ELASTIC:
Cut the length of the elastic so that it is 1 in/2.5 cm smaller than the recipient's waist measurement.

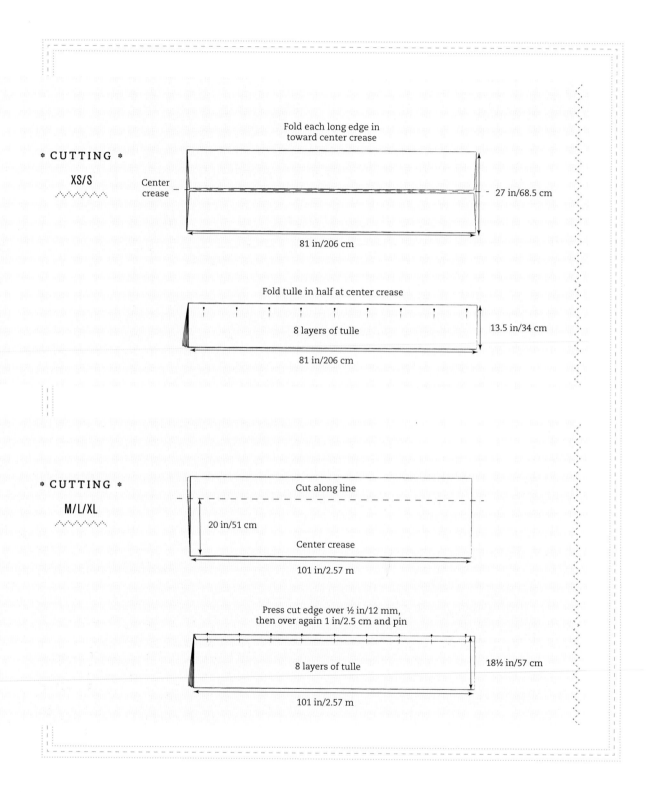

✶ CUTTING ✶

XS/S

Fold each long edge in
toward center crease

Center
crease

27 in/68.5 cm

81 in/206 cm

Fold tulle in half at center crease

8 layers of tulle

13.5 in/34 cm

81 in/206 cm

✶ CUTTING ✶

M/L/XL

Cut along line

20 in/51 cm

Center crease

101 in/2.57 m

Press cut edge over ½ in/12 mm,
then over again 1 in/2.5 cm and pin

8 layers of tulle

18½ in/57 cm

101 in/2.57 m

Assemble

STEP 1: SKIRT

A *Elastic casing:* For sizes XS and S, sew a seam ¾ in/2 cm from the center crease. For sizes M, L, and XL, edge stitch along the inner folded edge of the casing.

B *All sizes:* Trim the short edges of the Skirt so that all the layers are even.

C Place a safety pin into one end of the elastic and guide elastic through casing, being careful not to let the other end of the elastic slip all the way inside; hold it or pin it in place.

D Fold Skirt in half, align the short edges, and pin together. Beginning at the casing edge, sew a seam with ½-in/12-mm seam allowance, stopping 1½ in/4 cm from the upper edge; backstitch. Move down 5 in/12 cm below stopping point; continue sewing seam to lower edge. This will create an opening in the Skirt layers, so that you can decorate and fill the skirt as desired. *(See illustration below.)*

E Turn Skirt **right**-side out, so that the seam allowance is inside the Skirt.

STEP 2: FINISHING

A This is the fun part. Through the opening left in the seam, decorate and fill your Skirt with flower petals and leaves. Make sure that the filling is between the two outer layers of tulle.

B If you want to add a bit more interest, using white glue and a sponge brush, glue glitter on some petals and let them dry completely. Take another petal or leaf and position it inside the tulle, placing a dab of glue from glue gun on the outer layer. Then place the glittered petal on top of the glue, on the outside of the skirt, sandwiching the tulle in between. Let all the glue dry completely.

C When you have finished adding the decorations, turn Skirt inside out and sew the opening closed with a ½-in/12-mm seam allowance, then turn **right**-side out.

D Tie the ribbon into a pretty bow and tack it to casing at the Skirt seam. You can either sew or glue the ribbon in place.

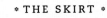

❋ THE SKIRT ❋

STEP **1D**

Fold skirt in half

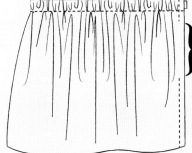

Leave a 5-in/12-cm opening

Align edges and stitch together with ½-in/12-mm seam allowance

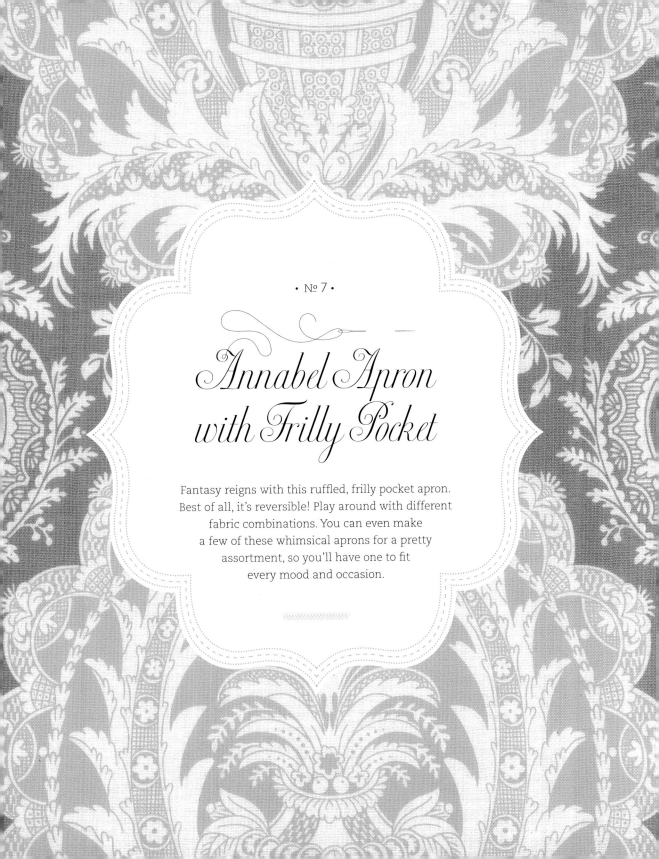

· № 7 ·

Annabel Apron
with Frilly Pocket

Fantasy reigns with this ruffled, frilly pocket apron.
Best of all, it's reversible! Play around with different
fabric combinations. You can even make
a few of these whimsical aprons for a pretty
assortment, so you'll have one to fit
every mood and occasion.

FINISHED SIZE OF APRON (not including ties)

❀ **XS AND S:** 12½ in/32 cm long by 21 in/53 cm at widest point

❀ **M, L, AND XL:** 13½ in/34 cm long by 22 in/56 cm at widest point

1 Printed mid-weight cotton fabric (45 in/114 cm wide) for
Apron (fabric A) and a coordinating fabric (fabric B):

SIZE	XS AND S	M, L, AND XL
Fabric A	1 yd/ 1 m	1⅛ yd/ 1.1 m
Fabric B	½ yd/ 45 cm	⅝ yd/ 60 cm

2 Coordinating thread

FROM THE SEWING BASKET:

❀ Scissors (for use with paper and fabric)

❀ Tracing paper (optional)

❀ Pencil (optional)

❀ Water-soluble fabric marker or chalk pencil

❀ Turning tool or thread and a large hand-sewing needle

❀ Small safety pin

❀ Small gauge string or crochet cotton

❀ Pins

❀ Ruler

Cutting

Cut out (or trace with tracing paper and pencil) the Apron pattern piece that is provided in the front pocket of this book, in the size you want to make.

FROM FABRIC A:

Cut 1 Apron piece, *on the fold*. After cutting out the Apron piece, clip a ¼-in/6-mm notch at the lower edge of the fold.

FOR THE RUFFLE:

SIZE	XS AND S	M, L, AND XL
Cut 2 rectangles (L by W)	4½ by 41 in/ 11 by 104 cm	5 by 44 in/ 12 by 112 cm

FOR THE WAIST TIE:

SIZE	XS AND S	M, L, AND XL
Cut 1 rectangle (L by W)	2¼ by 21 in/ 5.5 by 53 cm	2¾ by 25 in/ 7 by 63.5 cm
Cut 1 rectangle (L by W)	2¼ by 32 in/ 5.5 by 81 cm	2¾ by 36 in/ 7 by 91 cm

FOR POCKET AND POCKET TIE:

SIZE	XS AND S	M, L, AND XL
Pocket: Cut 1 rectangle (L by W)	3½ by 12¾ in/ 9 by 32 cm	4 by 13½ in/ 10 by 34 cm
Tie: Cut 1 rectangle (L by W)	1 by 24 in/ 2.5 by 61 cm	1 by 25 in/ 2.5 by 63.5 cm

FROM FABRIC B:

Cut 1 Apron piece, *on the fold*. After cutting out the Apron piece, clip a ¼-in/6-mm notch at the lower edge of the fold. With a fabric marker or chalk pencil, transfer the pocket outline from the Apron pattern piece to the **right** side of fabric.

FOR THE WAIST TIE:

SIZE	XS AND S	M, L, AND XL
Cut 1 rectangle (L by W)	2¼ by 21 in/ 5.5 by 53 cm	2¾ by 25 in/ 7 by 63.5 cm
Cut 1 rectangle (L by W)	2¼ by 32 in/ 5.5 by 81 cm	2¾ by 36 in/ 7 by 91 cm

STEP 1: POCKET

A Fold and press the Pocket Tie in half lengthwise, **right** sides together. Sew a seam with a ¼-in/6-mm seam allowance, and then run a second row of stitching right next to the first seam, a little less than ¼ in/6 mm from the raw edge. Trim the seam allowance to ⅛ in/3 mm. If you have a turning tool, use this to turn the Pocket Tie **right**-side out. (If you don't have a turning tool, thread a large hand-sewing needle with 2 lengths of thread that will extend at least 3 in/7.5 cm past the ends of both Ties. Draw the threaded needle through the tube, making sure to leave about 3 in/7.5 cm of thread exposed at each end. Stitch through the end of the tube that doesn't have the needle. Tie a large knot in the thread at this end and work the tube over the stitched end to get the turning process started. Pull the needle end of the thread, while continuing to work the knotted end through the tube, until the tube is **right**-side out. Trim off the stitched end and discard the thread.) Press tube flat. Put a small safety pin on one end of the tube and set aside.

B *Hem short ends of Pocket:* With Pocket piece **wrong**-side up, fold and press each short end up ¼ in/6 mm, then fold and press each end another ¼ in/6 mm. Edge stitch along inner folded edge of hem.

C *Tie Casing:* With Pocket piece **wrong**-side up, fold and press one long edge up ¼ in/6 mm, then fold up that edge ½ in/12 mm, and press. Edge stitch along inner folded edge of casing. Work the Pocket Tie through the casing, using the safety pin. Once Pocket Tie is drawn through the casing, remove safety pin and knot each end.

D *Attach Pocket:* With Pocket piece **wrong**-side up, fold and press the raw edge up ½ in/12 mm. Pin this folded edge over the pocket marking on fabric B Apron piece. Edge stitch Pocket in place, along this folded edge. Secure both top corners of the Pocket with a ⅜-in-/1-cm-long stitch. (*See illustration.*) Gently pull Pocket tie to gather center and tie in a bow.

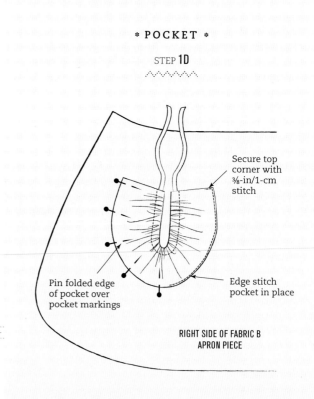

* POCKET *

STEP 1D

Secure top corner with ⅜-in/1-cm stitch

Pin folded edge of pocket over pocket markings

Edge stitch pocket in place

RIGHT SIDE OF FABRIC B APRON PIECE

STEP 2: RUFFLE

A Align both Ruffle pieces, with **right** sides together. Sew 1 of the short ends together with a ¼-in/ 6-mm seam allowance, so you now have 1 long Ruffle piece. Press seam open. Press Ruffle in half lengthwise with **right** sides together and sew each short end closed with a ¼-in/6-mm seam allowance. Turn Ruffle **right**-side out, aligning raw edges; press flat.

B Along the raw edge, work Gathering Method Two *(see page 24)*. Pin the Ruffle to fabric A Apron piece, along the outside curved edge. Align the Ruffle seam at the center Front lower edge notch, then pin the ends of the Ruffle ½ in/12 mm down from upper edge. Pull string to gather Ruffle to fit the curved Apron edge. Pin and distribute the gathers evenly. Baste Ruffle piece to Apron, ⅜ in/1 cm from raw edge, being careful not to stitch over the gathering string. Remove string and discard.

C With fabric A Apron piece **right**-side up, place fabric B Apron piece on top, with **right** sides together, and the Ruffle sandwiched between the layers. Align edges and pin along the outside curved edge, leaving upper edge open. Sew pieces together with a ½-in/12-mm seam allowance along curved edge. Clip the seam allowance along the curved edge, being careful to not clip the seam. Turn Apron **right**-side out through opening and press. Baste upper edge opening together, ¼ in/6 mm from edge, so the Apron layers won't shift when you are attaching the Waist Ties.

STEP 3: WAIST TIES

A Align both fabric A Waist Tie pieces along one short end and sew together with a ¼-in/6-mm seam allowance. Press seam open. Repeat for fabric B Waist Tie pieces.

B Fold each joined Waist Tie piece in half, matching at the short ends. With a ruler and fabric marker or chalk pencil, make a mark 1½ in/4 cm from end, along one long raw edge. Place the ruler at an angle on the end of the Waist Tie, line up the mark just made on the raw edge with the end of the other long raw edge, and draw a straight line. Cut along this line, to create the pointed Waist Tie ends. The edge with the point is the top edge and the opposite edge is the bottom edge of the Waist Tie. *(See illustration on page 86.)*

C With **right** sides together, match up both Waist Tie pieces along all edges and align seams. Working along the bottom edge on the longer piece of the Waist Tie, with a ruler and fabric marker, measure out from the join seam 12 in/30.5 cm for sizes XS and S, 13 in/33 cm for sizes M, L, and XL and make a mark; clip a ¼-in/6-mm notch at this mark on bottom edge of the Waist Tie. *(See illustration on page 86.)*

D Keeping Waist Tie pieces **right** sides together, pin edges. Sew around raw edges with a ⅜-in/1-cm seam allowance. Start at the notch made in Waist Tie and continue sewing until the Waist Tie join seam is reached, pivoting at each corner and leaving seam open between notch and seam.

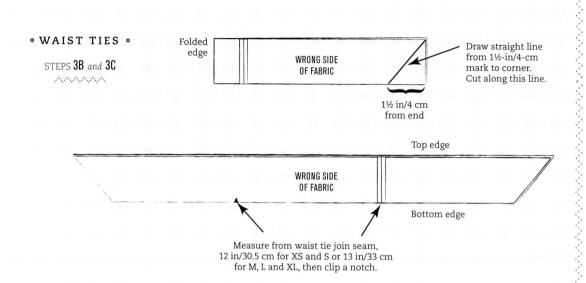

✻ WAIST TIES ✻

STEPS **3B** *and* **3C**

Folded edge

WRONG SIDE OF FABRIC

Draw straight line from 1½-in/4-cm mark to corner. Cut along this line.

1½ in/4 cm from end

Top edge

WRONG SIDE OF FABRIC

Bottom edge

Measure from waist tie join seam, 12 in/30.5 cm for XS and S or 13 in/33 cm for M, L and XL, then clip a notch.

Trim off seam allowance at the corners and turn the Waist Tie **right**-side out. Carefully, push out the corners and points using a turning tool, or the tip of a pair of scissors or knitting needle. Press Waist Tie flat, and then press the opening raw edges under ⅜ in/1 cm, lining up the folded edges.

E   Lay Apron piece flat, with fabric A side facing up. Place fabric B side of Waist Tie facedown on fabric A side of Apron. Unfold the Waist Tie opening seam allowance and align the raw edge with the top raw edge of the Apron, and pin in place. Sew together with a ⅜-in/1-cm seam allowance.

F   Turn Apron over, so that the fabric B side is facing up, and fold the fabric A side of the Waist Tie over, enclosing the raw edges and covering the stitches from the other side. Pin opening closed. Edge stitch around the entire Waist Tie, closing the opening on this side.

Accessories

· № 8 ·

Hadley Headband

Made with faux flowers, these floral adornments
will never wilt or fade. They're so easy to whip up
that you could easily make different styles
for each girl in your world.

Materials

1 3 to 6 artificial flower stems with leaves

2 1 inexpensive ½-in/12-mm plastic headband (with no teeth on the inside)

FROM THE CRAFT CABINET:

❋ Dual-temperature glue gun and glue sticks

Assemble

A Remove the flower heads and leaves from the stems of the flowers. Discard the stems.

B Using the lower temperature on the dual-temperature glue gun, glue the leaves to the inside and outside of Headband, overlapping the ends of the leaves so the Headband is completely covered. Let glue dry completely. (*See illustration.*)

C Beginning at the top center of the leaf-covered Headband, glue the flower heads in place. Let glue dry completely.

❋ **ASSEMBLE** ❋

STEP **B**

Glue leaves to headband

Overlap ends of leaves to completely cover headband

9

Penelope Ruffle-Top Purse

This pocketbook, or "book a pock," as my sister Shana
called it, is everything a girl could want in a purse.
The feminine ruffled top and small size make it
a great carryall for a frill-conscious little girl.

FINISHED SIZE OF PURSE (not including handles)

❁ 10½ in/26.5 cm wide at top by 9 in/23 cm tall by 3¼ in/8.3 cm deep

Materials

1 ⅝ yd/57 cm printed mid-weight cotton fabric (45 in/114 cm wide) for Purse, Strap, and Ruffle

2 ⅓ yd/30 cm coordinating mid-weight cotton fabric (45 in/114 cm wide) for Lining

3 ⅜ yd/35 cm heavyweight sew-in interfacing (we used HTC Ultra Firm)

4 Coordinating thread

FROM THE SEWING BASKET:

❁ Scissors (for use with paper and fabric)

❁ Tracing paper (optional)

❁ Pencil (optional)

❁ Pins

❁ Water-soluble fabric marker or chalk pencil

❁ Ruler

❁ Seam ripper

Cutting

Cut out (or trace with tracing paper and pencil) the Purse pattern piece that is provided in the front pocket of this book.

FROM THE PURSE FABRIC:

Cut 2 Purse pieces, *on the fold*. After cutting out the Purse pieces, clip notches where indicated on pattern.

Cut 2 rectangles 20 by 3¾ in/50 by 9.5 cm, for Straps.

Cut 1 rectangle 44 by 2½ in/112 by 6 cm, for Ruffle.

FROM THE LINING FABRIC:

Cut 2 Purse pieces, *on the fold*. After cutting out the Purse pieces, clip notches where indicated on pattern.

FROM THE INTERFACING:

Cut 2 Purse pieces, *on the fold*. After cutting out the Purse pieces, clip notches where indicated on pattern.

Cut 2 rectangles 20 by ⅞ in/50 by 2.1 cm, for Strap.

STEP 1: APPLY INTERFACING/SEW STRAPS

A   Lay 1 Purse piece, **wrong**-side up, on a flat surface; place a Purse interfacing piece on top, aligning all edges and pin together. Baste the interfacing to the purse fabric ¼ in/6 mm from edge. Repeat with other Purse and Purse interfacing pieces.

B   Fold Straps in half, lengthwise with **wrong** sides together and press. Open up, and then fold each raw edge in toward center crease and press. Unfold one edge and place Strap interfacing along center crease. Refold edge over interfacing and fold strap along center crease; press.

C   Pin the long edge of Strap closed and topstitch ⅛ in/3 mm from the folded edge, closing the Strap so that it can't be unfolded. Then topstitch ⅛ in/3 mm from the fold on opposite long edge. Repeat for other Strap. Set aside.

STEP 2: RUFFLE AND PURSE

A Align both short ends of the Ruffle piece, with **right** sides together; with a fabric marker or chalk pencil, place a mark at fold (center of Ruffle). Sew ends together with a ¼-in/6-mm seam allowance; Ruffle is joined in a loop. Press seam open. Fold Ruffle in half lengthwise, with **wrong** sides together; align the raw edges and press. Using Gathering Method One *(see page 24)*, run basting stitches along raw edge and gather.

B *Purse Seam:* Place both Purse pieces with **right** sides together; align all the raw edges and pin both sides and bottom together. Sew sides and bottom together with a ½-in/12-mm seam allowance. Clip off the bottom corners and press seams open.

C *Gussets:* Fold one side seam down to meet the bottom seam; this will form a triangle. With a ruler and fabric marker or chalk pencil, draw a line straight across the side seam at the notches. Pin and sew along line. Clip off the triangle, leaving ½-in/12-mm seam allowance. Repeat on other side. *(See illustration.)*

D Turn Purse **right**-side out and slip Ruffle piece over bag. Align Purse top raw edge with Ruffle raw edges, making sure the folded edge of the Ruffle is pointed toward the lower edge of the Purse. Match up Ruffle seam with one of the Purse side seams and the mark at the center of the ruffle with the opposite side seam, and pin. Distribute gathers evenly along top edge, pinning as needed. Baste Ruffle to bag, ⅜ in/1 cm from edge.

E *Attach Straps:* With Purse still **right**-side out, align end of one Strap along upper edge of Purse, placing it between 2 of the notches; pin in place. Being careful to not twist the Strap, place the opposite end of same Strap between the other set of notches on the same side of Purse (Back or Front) and pin. The Ruffle will be between the Purse and the Strap. Baste strap ends in place, ⅜ in/1 cm from edge. Repeat on other side of Purse.

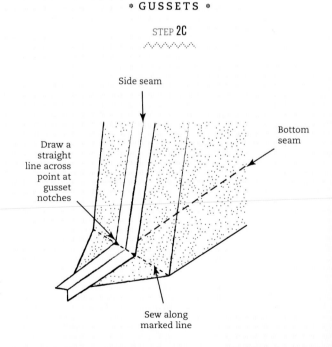

❋ GUSSETS ❋

STEP **2C**

Side seam

Bottom seam

Draw a straight line across point at gusset notches

Sew along marked line

STEP 3: LINING AND FINISHING

A Follow step 2B to join Purse Lining pieces, but, instead of stitching across the entire bottom edge, leave an opening about 6 in/15 cm long in that seam. Clip off the corners and press seams open. Then press bottom opening raw edges up ½ in/12 mm.

B Follow step 2C to make the Gussets in Lining.

C With Purse **right**-side out and Lining inside out, slip Lining over Purse (**right** sides are together). Make sure to keep Ruffle and Straps sandwiched between Purse and Lining. Match up side seams on both Purse and Lining pieces, then pin together along top edge. Sew the top edge together with a ½-in/12-mm seam allowance.

D Pull the Purse through the Lining opening, turning Lining **right**-side out. Align the folded edges of the Lining opening and edge stitch opening closed. Slip the Lining inside Purse and pull the Ruffle and Straps above the top edge of the Purse. Press along top edge.

E Topstitch around Purse opening ¼ in/6 mm below Purse/Ruffle seam. Remove any visible basting stitching from the Ruffle with a seam ripper.

Bonnie

SIS BOOM
COLLECTION

10

Chloe Paper Doll Overnight Bag

Sporting a paper doll on your overnight sack is pretty darn cool, or so we've been told by the girls of the Sis Boom fan club. With all the great ink-jet printer fabrics on the market, this is a simple project to complete. Use a vintage or contemporary paper doll, and make a pretty background from decorative scrapbook paper, wrapping paper, or fabric. Then, choose your dolly's skirt from any sort of fancy fabric and add some ribbon to finish it off.

FINISHED SIZE OF BAG (not including tie) ✤ 17 by 12½ in/43 by 32 cm

Materials

1 ¾ yd/70 cm printed mid-weight cotton fabric
   (45 in/114 cm wide) for Bag and Tie

2 Paper doll or image of paper doll and background

3 8½ by 11 in/20 by 29 cm ink-jet printer fabric, in white or cream

4 Coordinating thread

5 Scrap of decorative fabric (satin, or lightweight velvet; approximately 8 by 4 in/20 by 10 cm)
   for dolly Skirt

6 ¾ yd/70 cm ribbon (⅛ in/1 cm wide)

FROM THE SEWING BASKET:

✤ Scissors (for use with fabric)

✤ Ruler

✤ Water-soluble fabric marker or chalk pencil

✤ Hand-sewing needle or hot-glue gun and glue sticks

✤ Pins

✤ Turning tool or the tip of a pair of scissors or knitting needle

✤ Safety pin

Note: This bag may not be fully washable. It depends on the type of ink-jet printer fabric, the doll's skirt fabric, and how you attach the skirt to the bag. Please keep this in mind and follow the manufacturer's instructions for care.

Cutting

FROM THE BAG FABRIC:

Cut 1 rectangle, 21 by 26 in/53 by 66 cm. Fold rectangle in half widthwise, with **right** sides together, matching the shorter raw edges.

With a ruler and fabric marker or chalk pencil, make 2 marks along the 21-in/53-cm raw edge as follows: Make 1 mark 6¼ in/16 cm from the top edge.

Make 1 mark 7¼ in/18.5 cm from the top edge. *(See illustration.)*

Clip small notches into the seam allowances at these marks.

Cut 1 cross-grain binding strip, 2 by 40 in/5 by 102 cm, for Tie.

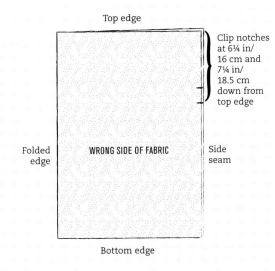

Top edge

Clip notches at 6¼ in/ 16 cm and 7¼ in/ 18.5 cm down from top edge

Folded edge

WRONG SIDE OF FABRIC

Side seam

Bottom edge

Assemble

STEP 1: TRANSFER IMAGE TO FABRIC/ATTACH TO BAG.

A   You can use an image you already have or one you create on your computer and print it onto the ink-jet printer fabric, or you can copy an image onto the ink-jet printer fabric. Please follow the ink-jet printer fabric manufacturer's instructions to transfer your image to fabric.

B   Place the ink-jet printer fabric with its completed image **wrong** side facing up, then turn edges of fabric over ⅜ in/1 cm on all sides and press.

C   *Dolly Skirt: Note:* For the Skirt, when the instructions say *attach*, either sew or hot glue that item in place. Place dolly Skirt fabric **right**-side up on a flat surface and *attach* ribbon to one 8-in/20-cm raw edge. Fold each of the shorter (4-in/10-cm) ends under and press. Using Gathering Method

One *(see page 24)*, gather the other 8-in/20-cm raw edge, so that it's approximately the same width as the dolly's waist and *attach* it to the image. *Attach* each of the folded under ends to the image, so the Skirt fans out at the lower edge. *Attach* a small length of ribbon to cover the waist of the Skirt. Tie the remaining ribbon into a bow and *attach* at the center of the waist ribbon.

Placement of image

Top edge

RIGHT SIDE OF FABRIC

2 ⅜ in/
6 cm
from
folded
edge

2 ⅞ in/
7 cm
from side
seam

2 in/5 cm from lower edge

D   Fold Bag piece in half widthwise, with **wrong** sides together. Place image, **right**-side up, on folded Bag piece. Center the image fabric across the folded width (allowing for ½-in/12-mm seam allowance), approximately 2 in/5 cm up from lower edge. *(See illustration.)* Pin in place to only 1 layer of the folded Bag piece. Unfold Bag and edge stitch image in place.

STEP 2: ASSEMBLE BAG

A   Fold Bag piece in half widthwise, with **right** sides together, aligning raw edges. Pin, leaving upper edge open. Beginning at the bottom of the Bag, sew seam with a ½-in/12-mm seam allowance, pivoting at the corner and continuing up the side to the first set of notches; backstitch to end seam. Move the fabric and begin sewing at the second set of notches, then continue sewing to upper edge, leaving a 1-in/2.5-cm opening in the side seam between the notches. *(See illustration on page 105.)* Clip off the bottom corners and press side seam open. Finish side seam and bottom edges in your preferred method *(see page 23)*.

B   Sew the seam allowances flat at the side seam opening, by topstitching ⅛ in/3 mm from each folded edge. *(See illustration on page 105.)*

C   With Bag inside out, fold the upper edge over ½ in/12 mm and press. Fold over and press the top edge again 3½ in/9 cm from first fold. Pin top edge in place as needed, then edge stitch along the inner folded edge. With a fabric marker or chalk pencil, draw a straight line 1¼ in/3 cm up from stitched edge; stitch along this line to create the Tie casing. Turn Bag **right**-side out, then carefully push out corners with a turning tool or the tip of a pair of scissors or knitting needle and press.

STEP 3: FINISHING

A *Tie:* Press the binding strip into double-fold binding *(see page 20)*.

B Pin the 2 long folded edges together and topstitch closed, ⅛ in/3 mm from the edge. Topstitch ⅛ in/3 mm from opposite edge (fold), to complete the Bag Tie.

C Place a safety pin in one end of the Tie and thread it through the Bag casing. Align the Tie ends and knot them together.

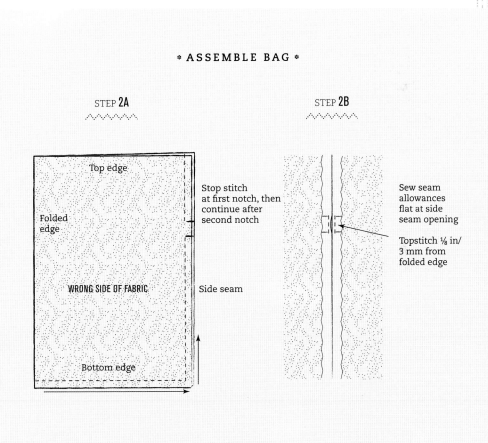

❁ ASSEMBLE BAG ❁

STEP **2A**

Top edge

Folded edge

WRONG SIDE OF FABRIC

Bottom edge

Stop stitch at first notch, then continue after second notch

Side seam

STEP **2B**

Sew seam allowances flat at side seam opening

Topstitch ⅛ in/ 3 mm from folded edge

· № 11 ·

Girls' "Ambassador of Goodwill" Badges

These fancy glittered badges make a fun and friendship-
strengthening party activity. They are a cinch to make—
just print out a few inspiring phrases, decorate the chipboard
die-cut frames with glitter, glue them together, and
add seam binding for hanging around the neck.
Just be sure you make enough for every girl to
receive one, so no one is left out!

FINISHED SIZE OF BADGES

❋ Badge sizes will vary depending on the number and size of the die-cut frames used.

Materials

1 8½-by-11-in/21.5-by-28-cm card stock paper for printing (You can print multiple phrases on one sheet of paper.)

2 2 or 3 chipboard die-cut frames and frame centers per badge (see "Resources," page 172)

3 Fine glitter in various colors

4 3 to 4 yd/2.75 to 3.75 m Hug Snug rayon seam binding (½ in/12 mm) per badge in 2 different colors (see "Resources," page 172); plus additional seam binding (optional)

FROM THE SEWING BASKET:

❋ Scissors (for use with paper and fabric)

FROM THE CRAFT CABINET:

❋ Newspapers to cover your work area

❋ Fine-grit sandpaper

❋ ½-in/12-mm sponge brush

❋ White glue

❋ Hot-glue gun and glue sticks

Note: Here are a few sample phrases to get you started.
Feel free to come up with your own.
❋ Biggest Heart
❋ Friendliest Smile
❋ Lucky Girl
❋ Happy Camper
❋ Adored
❋ Great Friend

STEP 1: PRINT PHRASES AND PREP FRAMES

A Using a computer printer, print out the phrase(s) that you want to use for the badges on card stock, making sure the printed phrase(s) will fit inside the largest frame. Cover your work surface with newspaper.

B Lightly rub the fine sandpaper around the front of each frame and frame center that will be used. (This will give the smooth chipboard some texture, to help the glitter adhere to the surface more easily.) Remove sanding dust from pieces with a damp cloth.

C Using sponge brush, coat the front of each frame and frame center with white glue, and then cover them generously with glitter. Let them dry completely. Shake off excess glitter. Add a second coat of glue and glitter, if the frame front isn't completely covered. Let dry completely.

D Cut seam binding into 45-in/114-cm lengths (2 pieces, 1 of each color for each badge). Optional Fringe: Cut 5 pieces of seam binding, each 10 in/25.5 cm long. These may be added to the lower edge of badge, if desired.

STEP 2: FINISHING

A Once pieces are completely dry, they're ready to be assembled into a badge, using the hot-glue gun. Choose and cut out the phrase you want, then center the phrase inside the largest frame. Once it's centered, trace around the outside edge of the frame, and then cut out the phrase along the traced lines. Turn the frame over, with back of frame facing up, and place small beads of hot glue all around the frame. Place the phrase, with the back of the phrase facing up, onto the glue and align along all of the edges of the frame.

B Decide on the layout of the frames and frame centers for your finished badge. You will need to place an open frame piece at the top of the badge, so you can attach the long pieces of seam binding through it. Starting with the top frame piece, hot-glue the back of next piece to the lower edge of it, overlapping them the width of the pieces. Continue to glue the pieces together as desired, working from the upper edge to the lower edge of the badge. If optional fringe on the lower edge of the badge is desired, hold the 5 pieces of fringe together and fold them in half. Slightly fan out the ends, then glue the folded end of the fringe to the back at the lower edge of the badge. On the back, cover the folded end of the fringe with a frame center, if desired. Let the glue dry completely.

C Holding the 2 pieces of 45-in/114-cm seam binding together, fold them in half. Insert the folded edge through the top frame; wrap the loose ends around the frame and slip them through the loop formed by the folded edge. Bring the ends up and tighten the loop around the frame. Tie all of the loose ends together in a knot, adjusting the length for the recipient.

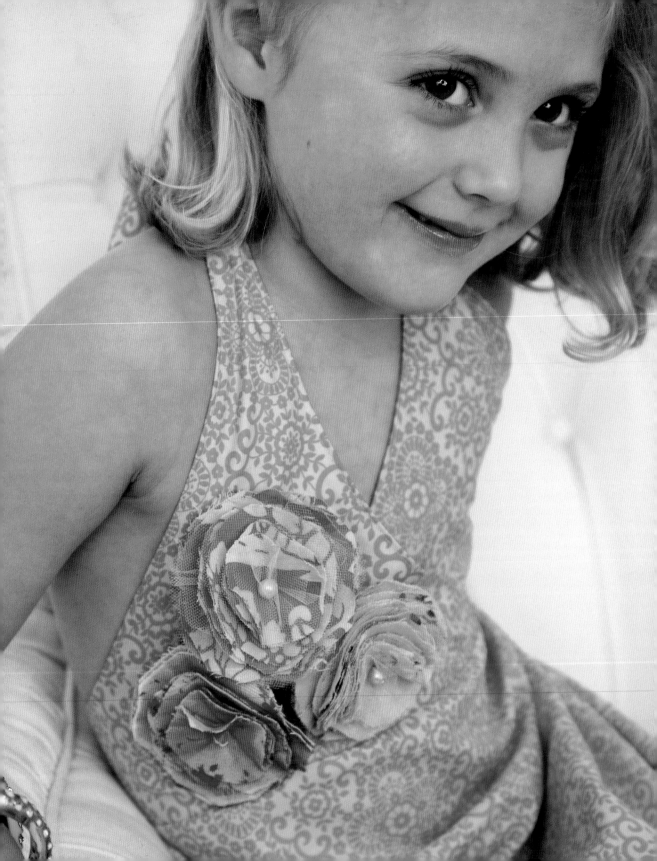

• № 12 •

Fiona Fabric Flower Pin/Barrette

This clever accessory can be made into a pin and/or a barrette. Wear it alone, or group several together for an over-the-top feminine look. The polished pearl bead in the center balances the roughness of the raw fabric edges for an effect that is both elegant and casual. This beautiful design was contributed by Carla Hageman Crim.

FINISHED SIZE OF FLOWERS

❀ **SMALL FLOWER** 3 in/7.5 cm diameter

❀ **LARGE FLOWER** 4 in/10 cm diameter

1 ⅜ yd/35 cm printed mid-weight cotton fabric (45 in/114 cm wide) for flower(s)

2 1 roll (25 yd/23 m) tulle (6 in/15 cm wide)

3 Coordinating thread

4 1 faux pearl bead for each flower

5 1 barrette and/or 1 pin back (1 in/2.5 cm long) for each flower

FROM THE SEWING BASKET:

❀ Scissors (for use with paper and fabric)

❀ Tracing paper (optional)

❀ Pencil (optional)

❀ Pins

❀ Large hand-sewing needle

FROM THE CRAFT CABINET:

❀ Spray starch

❀ Hot-glue gun and glue sticks (optional)

Note: The fabric amount provided is enough to make 2 large flowers, 4 small flowers, or 1 large and 2 small flowers. The roll of tulle is enough to make approximately 10 large flowers.

Cutting

Cut out (or trace with tracing paper and pencil) the petals pieces that are provided in the front pocket of this book.

FROM FLOWER FABRIC:

Cut 8 rectangles, each 6 by 11 in/15 by 28 cm, separated into 2 stacks of 4 rectangles each.

Lay 1 rectangle on a flat surface, then unroll 2 layers of tulle on top of the fabric. Place the second rectangle on top of the tulle and unroll 2 more layers of tulle. Continue the layering of fabric and tulle until you have a stack of 4 layers of fabric and 8 layers of tulle.

Pin pattern pieces to 1 stack of fabric and tulle; use pieces A through E for a large flower and pieces C through E for a small flower. Cut out the pieces, keeping pieces of the same size stacked together.

Repeat the above 2 steps with the second set of fabric rectangles.

Assemble

STEP 1: MAKE FLOWERS

A Thread the needle, align both ends of the thread and tie a knot. Keeping all the layers together, insert the needle in the center back (first fabric piece) of the largest stack. Turn the stack so that the tulle side is facing up and continue to add the stacks in alphabetical order, inserting the needle into the center of each stack.

B After the smallest stack is added, use the needle to draw the thread through the pearl bead. Reinsert the needle through the center of the flower and pull the thread all the way through to the *back* of the largest stack. Tie a knot, and then cut the thread near the eye of the needle; the thread tail will be used in the next step.

C Submerge the flower in a basin of water. Form a bell shape with the petals in your hand and squeeze out as much water as possible. Tie the thread tail to a towel bar or shower curtain rod and let the flower hang dry.

D After an hour or so, spray the exposed surfaces of the damp flower with spray starch. Let flower dry overnight. When it is completely dry, separate and rotate the layers to fluff.

E Hot-glue or hand sew, using needle and thread, the barrette and/or pin back to the center back of the flower. If you want the option of having the flower be both a barrette and a pin, place the barrette at the center back of the flower, then place the pin back ½ in/12 mm above the barrette.

Bridget Banner with Pom-Poms

A banner with colorful fabric patches and pom-poms?
What's not to love? Brighten up your girl's bedroom by hanging
this banner over a desk, headboard, or dresser. Or take it a
step further and hang a banner around the entire perimeter
of her room. Feel free to customize by changing the
size of the banner pieces or adjusting the space
between the pieces. This is the perfect project
for using up those fabric scraps you
couldn't bear to throw away.

FINISHED SIZE OF BANNER (including ties) ❋ 5 by 132 in/20 cm by 3.35 m

Materials

1 20 assorted mid-weight cotton fabric scraps (each 5 by 6 in/12 by 15 cm) for Banner

2 ¼ yd/23 cm printed mid-weight cotton fabric (45 in/114 cm wide) for binding

3 ⅜ yd/35 cm fusible fleece (45 in/114 cm wide) for backing

4 3½ yd/3.2 m pom-pom fringe (⅜ in/1 cm wide)

5 Coordinating thread

FROM THE SEWING BASKET:

❋ Scissors (for use with fabric)

❋ Ruler

❋ Hand-sewing needle or hot-glue gun and glue sticks

❋ Water-soluble fabric marker or chalk pencil

❋ Pins

Cutting

FROM THE BANNER FABRICS:

Cut 40 rectangles, each 4½ by 2¾ in/11 by 7 cm.

FROM THE BINDING FABRIC:

Cut enough 2-in-/5-cm-wide cross-grain binding strips *(see page 22)*, so that, when pieced together, they measure 132 in/3.35 m long.

FROM THE FUSIBLE FLEECE:

Cut 40 rectangles, each 4½ by 2¾ in/11 by 7 cm.

FROM THE POM-POM FRINGE:

Cut 40 pieces, each 2¾ in/7 cm long.

Assemble

STEP 1: BANNER PIECES

A   Lay fusible fleece backing pieces on a flat surface, with fusible side facing up; place fabric Banner pieces on top of each fleece piece, with **right** side facing up. Fuse pieces together, following fusible fleece manufacturer's instructions.

B   Attach pom-pom fringe to the back of lower edge on each Banner piece, by sewing in place or using hot-glue gun. If using hot glue, let it dry completely before proceeding to the next step.

STEP 2: FINISHING

A   Join the cross-cut binding strips together, following the instructions on page 22. Then press the joined strip into double-fold binding *(see page 20)*.

B   Unfold binding entirely and place on flat surface with **right** side facing up. Using a ruler, measure in from each end 11 in/28 cm and make a mark with a fabric marker or chalk pencil on the top raw edge. Beginning at mark, working from left to right, place Banner pieces, **right** side facing up, in order as desired, on binding. Align the binding top raw edge with the top raw edge of the Banner pieces and pin them in place. The Banner pieces should be butted up against each other. *(Refer to illustration for "Happy Birthday Banner," step 2B, page 168.)*

C   Sew the Banner pieces to the binding with a ½-in/12-mm seam allowance. Trim the seam allowance on the Banner pieces to ⅛ in/3 mm.

D   Fold the binding to the front of the Banner, enclosing all raw edges. Begin at one end and pin the binding's folded edges together. Then pin the binding to Banner pieces so it covers the stitching made in step 2C; at opposite end of binding, pin folded edges together. Sew the binding ⅛ in/3 mm from folded edge, the entire length of the Banner. Press.

E   Knot each end of the binding, and hang the Banner in a special spot in your girl's bedroom.

· № 14 ·

Gigi Ruffled Pillow

This pretty pillow makes a great throw pillow for a bed
or a lovely accent for an overstuffed chair. Soft and comfy,
it's just right for lounging, or for curling up with at
bedtime. It looks great in a single fabric or in
a lovely mix of stripes and a floral.

FINISHED SIZE OF PILLOW ✽ 17 in/43 cm diameter by 7 in/18 cm high by 50 in/127 cm circumference

Materials

1 1⅜ yd/1.3 m of striped mid-weight cotton fabric (45 in/114 cm wide) for Top and Bottom

2 ⅝ yd/60 cm of coordinating mid-weight cotton fabric (45 in/114 cm wide) for Sides and Piping

3 3 yd/2.75 m of ⁶⁄₃₂-in/5-mm cotton filler cord

4 1 Dritz covered button kit (size 1⅛ in/2.8 cm diameter)

5 Coordinating thread

6 Fiberfill

FROM THE SEWING BASKET:

✽ Scissors (for use with paper and fabric)

✽ Tracing paper (optional)

✽ Pencil (optional)

✽ Pins

✽ Zipper foot for sewing machine

✽ Fine gauge string or crochet cotton

✽ Large tapestry needle

Cutting

Cut out (or trace with tracing paper and pencil) the Pillow Top/Bottom pattern piece that is provided in the front pocket of this book.

FROM TOP/BOTTOM FABRIC:

Fold fabric in half, **right** sides together, lining up the cut edges. Cut a total of 8 Pillow Top/Bottom pieces: 4 for Top, 4 for Bottom.

FROM SIDES AND PIPING FABRIC:

Cut 2 rectangles, 5½ by 26 in/14 by 66 cm. Fold each rectangle in half crosswise, aligning along the short ends, and clip a ¼-in/6-mm notch at both the upper and lower edge of the fold.

Cut enough 1⅝-in-/4.1-cm-wide bias binding strips (*see page 22*), so that, when pieced together, they measure 108 in/2.75 m long.

Save the scraps for making the fabric-covered buttons.

Assemble

STEP 1: PILLOW TOP, BOTTOM, AND SIDES

A   *Assemble Top and Bottom:* Place 2 Top/Bottom pieces, **right** sides together, aligning all edges. Pin along 1 of the straight edges, and then sew pieces together with a ½-in/12-mm seam allowance. Repeat with another set of 2 pieces. Lay the 2 joined pieces one on top of the other, **right** sides together, aligning all the raw edges. Pin along the 2 straight edges. Sew each of the straight edges together with ½-in/12-mm seam allowance; you now have a doughnut-shaped piece. Press all seams open. Repeat with the other 4 Top/Bottom pieces.

B   Use Gathering Method Two (*see page 24*) and sew around the outer edge of each of the Top/Bottom pieces. Sew around the inside edges using the same gathering method, but make the zigzag stitch length shorter, because the string will be staying in place on the inside edges. (*See illustration on page 126.*) Set both of these pieces aside. You will gather in step 2C.

C   *Sides:* Lay Side pieces **right** sides together; align all edges. Pin together both short ends. Sew short ends together with a ½-in/12-mm seam allowance to form a wide short tubular shape. Press seams open and set aside.

D   Join the bias binding strips together (*see page 22*).

STEP 1B

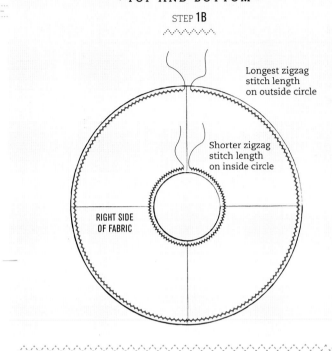

Longest zigzag
stitch length
on outside circle

Shorter zigzag
stitch length
on inside circle

RIGHT SIDE
OF FABRIC

STEP 2: ASSEMBLE PILLOW

A   Put zipper foot on sewing machine. With bias strip **wrong**-side up, place filler cord down the center of the bias strip. Fold the bias strip in half lengthwise. Align the raw edges, encasing the filler cord; pin. Sew the raw edges together, as close to the encased filler cord as possible. You will end up with about a ½-in/12-mm seam allowance from the raw edge to the stitching and the total width of the Piping should be about ⅞ in/2.2 cm. *(See illustration on page 127.)*

B   With Side piece **right**-side out, align Piping along one of the raw edges. Begin and end the Piping at one of the side seams, leaving about a 2-in/5-cm tail of Piping at the beginning. Pin Piping in place and baste to Side piece, ⅜ in/1 cm from the edge. *Note:* When you sew around the Side piece and arrive back at the beginning of the Piping, overlap the Piping while pulling the tail and the other end of the Piping up. The ends of the Piping need to be caught in the basting; you may want to backstitch over this point a second time. Trim the tails off the Piping. Repeat on other raw edge of Side piece. *(See illustration on page 127.)*

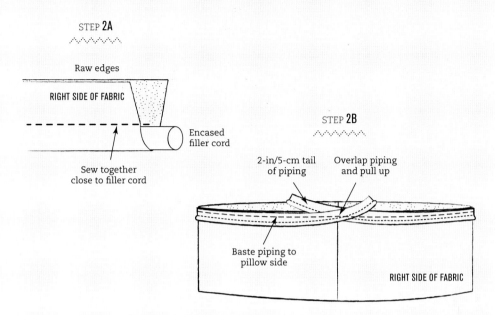

STEP **2A**

Raw edges

RIGHT SIDE OF FABRIC

Encased
filler cord

Sew together
close to filler cord

STEP **2B**

2-in/5-cm tail
of piping

Overlap piping
and pull up

Baste piping to
pillow side

RIGHT SIDE OF FABRIC

C Align the outside circular edge of one of the Top/Bottom pieces with one edge of the Side piece, **right** sides together; match up the Top/Bottom seams to the Pillow Side seams and notches and pin at these 4 points. Pull the string to gather the Top/Bottom outside edge; distribute the gathers evenly and pin all around. Sew together with a ½-in/12-mm seam allowance, sewing as close to the Piping as possible. Repeat with other Top/Bottom piece and attach to the other edge of Side piece.

D Remove the gathering string from both of the outer edges. Turn pillow **right**-side out through one of the inside openings.

STEP 3: FINISHING

A *Covered buttons:* Use the leftover fabric and follow the manufacturer's instructions to make the two covered buttons. Set them aside.

B Gather one inside circle edge as tightly as possible; when the covered button is over the center, it should cover all of the raw edges. Pull the loose ends of the zigzag threads inside (to the **wrong** side of the pillow) and knot them. Next, pull the ends of the gathering string inside and knot tightly. This side will now be referred to as the Bottom.

C Stuff the pillow with fiberfill, through the Top circular hole; do not overstuff. As you're stuffing the pillow, keep track of the Bottom string ends; once you are finished with stuffing, bring the Bottom string ends out through the Top circle.

D Gather the Top circle, as you did for the Bottom. Knot the zigzag thread loose ends and tuck them inside. Knot the string, trim so that the ends are even, and thread the tapestry needle with both ends together. While holding onto the Bottom string that is threaded outside the Top hole, push the needle down through the center of the pillow and out the Bottom hole. *(See illustration.)* Unthread the needle.

E With the Bottom of the pillow facing up, take one covered button and feed one of the top strings through the shank. Tie into a knot with the other top string, while pulling the string, so that the button sits flat inside the dimple created. Push the string end down inside the hole under the button. Repeat on the Top side of the pillow with the other button.

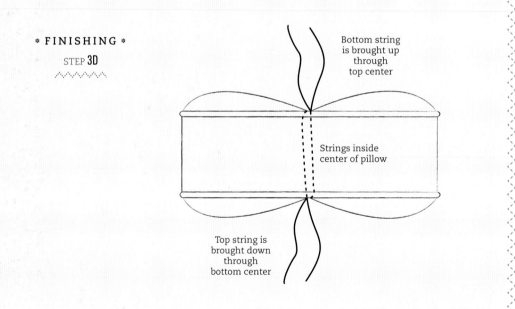

❋ **FINISHING** ❋

STEP **3D**

Bottom string is brought up through top center

Strings inside center of pillow

Top string is brought down through bottom center

· № 15 ·

Willow Small Pillow with Pom-Poms

This quick and fun project makes a fetching little gift for a special girl or her special dolly. You can use any type of button you wish, but fabric-covered buttons make these pillows oh-so fancy.

FINISHED SIZE OF PILLOW ❀ 7-in/18-cm square

∨∧∨

Materials

1 1 fat quarter (a piece of fabric cut into an 18-by-22-in/46-by-56-cm rectangle) of printed mid-weight cotton fabric for Pillow

2 1 yd/1 m pom-pom fringe (½ in/12 mm wide)

3 Coordinating thread

4 Fiberfill

5 1 Dritz covered button kit (⅞ in/2.2 cm diameter), or 2 buttons (each ⅞ in/2.2 cm diameter) of your choice

FROM THE SEWING BASKET:

❀ Scissors (for use with fabric)

❀ Water-soluble fabric marker or chalk pencil

❀ Pins

❀ Turning tool or the tip of a pair of scissors or knitting needle

❀ Hand-sewing needle

Cutting

FROM THE PILLOW FABRIC:

Fold fabric in half, **right** sides together, lining up short ends. Cut 2 (7¾-in/19.75-cm) squares. On the **right** side of each piece, mark the center of each square with a small dot, using fabric marker or chalk pencil. Save the scraps for making the fabric-covered buttons.

Assemble

STEP 1: PILLOW

A *Attach Fringe:* Place 1 Pillow piece, with **right** side facing up, on a flat surface. Beginning at a corner, pin straight edge of Fringe tape (the side without pom-poms) along the 4 raw edges of the pillow. *Note:* You will need to clip into the Fringe tape to go around the corners; be careful not to cut the Fringe tape apart. Overlap the ends of the Fringe tape at the first corner. Sew the tape in place ⅜ in/1 cm from the edge. *(See illustration.)*

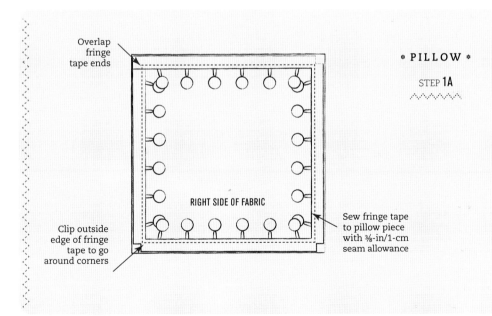

Overlap fringe tape ends

Clip outside edge of fringe tape to go around corners

RIGHT SIDE OF FABRIC

Sew fringe tape to pillow piece with ⅜-in/1-cm seam allowance

✳ **PILLOW** ✳

STEP **1A**

B Place the second Pillow piece on top of the first, with **right** sides together, making sure all the pom-poms are sandwiched in between the Pillow pieces. Align the raw edges and pin. Sew together with a ⅜-in/1-cm seam allowance, pivoting around each corner and leaving a 5-in/12.75-cm opening on one side for turning.

C Trim off corners; turn Pillow **right**-side out through opening. Gently push out corners with a turning tool or the tip of a pair of scissors or knitting needle and press. On the side of the opening that doesn't have the Fringe attached, turn under the raw edge ⅜ in/1 cm and press.

STEP 2: FINISHING

A Stuff the pillow with fiberfill, making sure not to overstuff. Using needle and thread, slip stitch the opening closed.

B *Buttons:* If using fabric-covered buttons, use the leftover fabric and follow the manufacturer's instructions to make them.

C Cut 2 pieces of thread the same length, and feed them both through the eye of the hand-sewing needle. Match up all the ends and tie a knot. You will have a total of 4 strands of thread. Insert the needle into the center mark on one side of the Pillow, and draw the needle through the Pillow and out the other side at the center mark. Repeat this action a couple of times, to create a dimple at the center of the Pillow. Take 1 button and thread onto the needle, pull it down the thread to the dimple just made. Insert needle into the dimple and pull out the other side of the Pillow. Thread the second button onto the needle and pull it down the thread to the dimple. Insert needle into the dimple again, pull it out the first side and knot the end. Be sure to hide the knot under the button.

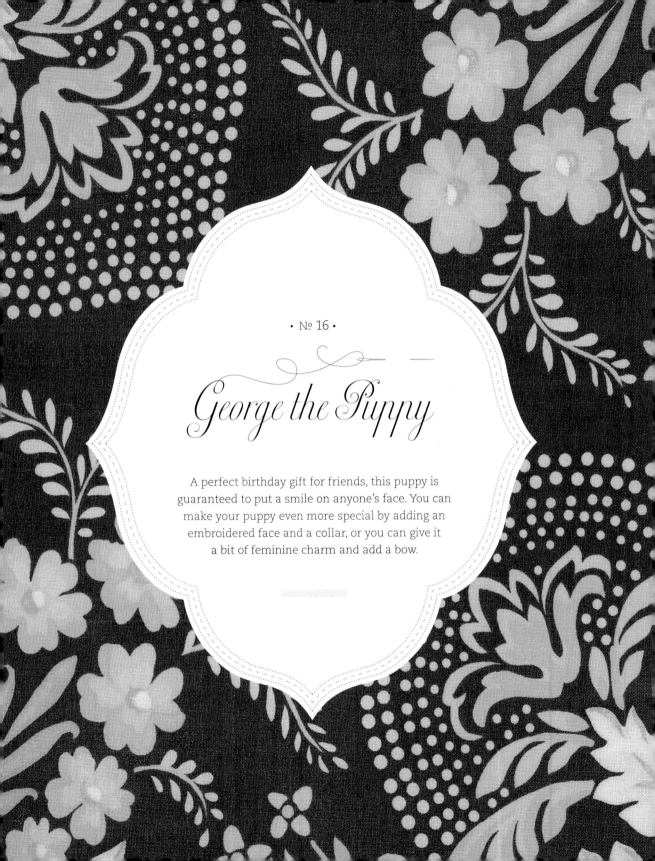

• № 16 •

George the Puppy

A perfect birthday gift for friends, this puppy is
guaranteed to put a smile on anyone's face. You can
make your puppy even more special by adding an
embroidered face and a collar, or you can give it
a bit of feminine charm and add a bow.

FINISHED SIZE OF PUPPY ❋ 14½ by 8½ in/37 by 20 cm

Materials

1 ¼ yd/23 cm printed mid-weight cotton fabric (45 in/114 cm wide) for Body

2 6-by-14-in/15-by-35.5-cm coordinating mid-weight cotton for Ears

3 Coordinating thread

4 Fiberfill

FROM THE SEWING BASKET:

❋ Scissors (for use with paper and fabric)

❋ Tracing paper (optional)

❋ Pencil (optional)

❋ Pins

❋ Hand-sewing needle

❋ Turning tool or the tip of a pair of scissors or knitting needle

❋ **BODY** ❋

STEP **2B**

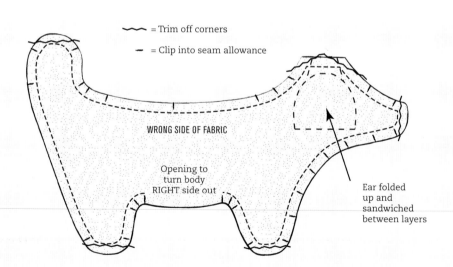

⌒⌒ = Trim off corners

— = Clip into seam allowance

WRONG SIDE OF FABRIC

Opening to
turn body
RIGHT side out

Ear folded
up and
sandwiched
between layers

 Cutting

Cut out (or trace with tracing paper and pencil) the Body and Ear pattern pieces that are provided in the front pocket of this book.

FROM THE BODY FABRIC:
Fold fabric in half, **right** sides together, lining up selvage edges. Cut 2 Body pieces. After cutting out the Body pieces, clip notches where indicated on pattern.

FROM THE EAR FABRIC:
Fold fabric in half, **right** sides together, lining up along the short ends. Cut a total of 4 Ear pieces.

 Assemble

STEP 1: EARS

A Place 2 Ear pieces, **right** sides together, aligning all edges and pin. Sew with a ¼-in/6-mm seam allowance around curved edge, leaving the flat end open. Repeat with the remaining 2 ear pieces.

B Clip the seam allowance around the curved edges. Turn ears **right**-side out and press flat.

STEP 2: BODY

A Place 1 Body piece, with **right** side facing up, on a flat surface. Place 1 Ear on top of the other, aligning raw edges. Place them between the notches on the head of the Body piece, aligning the raw edges of the Ears with the raw edge of the head. Baste the Ears in place, slightly less than ¼ in/6 mm from edge.

B Place second Body piece on top of the first, with **right** sides together; align all edges and pin together around edges. *Note:* Fold the Ears so that they are sandwiched inside the 2 Body pieces; they should only be sewn into the seam at the top of the head. Sew Body pieces together with a ¼-in/6-mm seam allowance, leaving an opening between the 2 notches at the belly. *(See illustration.)*

C Trim off corners and clip seam allowance on all the curved seams. Turn Body **right**-side out, through the opening. Gently push out all corners with a turning tool or the tip of a pair of scissors or knitting needle. Press the opening edges under ¼ in/6 mm.

D Stuff the Body firmly with fiberfill. Using needle and thread, slip stitch the opening closed.

• № 17 •

Genevieve
Patchwork Square Quilt

Easy enough for a beginning quilter, this patchwork quilt
is so much fun to make. Get creative with this project! The
quilt top is made from 64 squares, set in an 8-by-8 grid. You could
use 8 different fabrics and cut 8 squares from each, or 4 different
fabrics and cut 16 squares from each. In fact, you can
use any other number of fabrics, as long as you have
a total of 4 yd/3.75 m of fabric for the top.
There are so many options! This quilt
was created by Nancy Geaney.

FINISHED SIZE OF QUILT ✻ 60½-in/1.5-m square

Materials

1 4 yd/3.75 m total of printed mid-weight cotton fabric (45 in/114 cm wide) for top

2 4 yd/3.75 m of mid-weight cotton fabric (45 in/114 cm wide) for backing

3 ½ yd/45 cm of mid-weight cotton fabric (45 in/114 cm wide) for binding

4 Twin-bed size cotton batting or a 68-in/1.75-m square piece of cotton batting

5 Light-colored neutral 100-percent cotton thread for piecing

6 Coordinating 100-percent cotton thread for quilting (for stitch in the ditch or free-motion options only)

7 Coordinating embroidery floss (for hand-tied option only)

FROM THE SEWING BASKET:

✻ Scissors (for use with fabric)

✻ Rotary cutter and cutting mat (These are optional, but make cutting all those squares a lot easier.)

✻ Pins

✻ Hand-sewing needle

✻ Safety pins (optional)

✻ Clear ruler

✻ Darning foot for your sewing machine (for free-motion quilting option)

✻ Walking foot for your sewing machine (for stitch in the ditch option)

FROM THE CRAFT CABINET:

✻ Digital camera or graph paper and colored pencils (optional)

✻ Masking tape

✻ Quilt basting spray (temporary fabric adhesive)

Note: There are many options for how to finish your quilt. The quilt pictured on pages 140 and 147 was quilted by making a wavy free-motion quilting pattern throughout the entire quilt. If you want to do free-motion quilting, you can use any design you like. Other options for quilting include stitching in the ditch with a sewing machine, hand-tying the quilt, and even hand quilting. (Refer to "Getting Started," page 16, for quilting instructions.)

FROM THE QUILT TOP FABRICS:

Cut a total of 64 squares, each 8 in/20. 5 cm.

FROM THE BACKING FABRIC:

Cut 2 rectangles, each 68 by 34¼ in/175 by 87 cm.

FROM THE BINDING FABRIC:

Cut enough 2½-in-/6-cm-wide cross-grain binding strips (*see page 22*), so that, when pieced together, they measure 7¼ yd/6.6 m long.

STEP 1: TOP LAYOUT

A Depending on how many fabrics you choose for the Quilt Top, you need to decide how you want the squares to be pieced together. We have provided 2 options for the layout, one with 8 different fabrics and another with 4 different fabrics. *(See illustrations.)* These are just suggestions—feel free to play with different layout patterns. To try your own pattern, lay all of the squares for the Top on the floor or work table in an 8-by-8 grid; move them around until you're happy with the overall layout.

B Once you've decided on the layout, take a quick picture or draw your layout pattern on a piece of graph paper with colored pencils. That way, if the squares get moved or you lose your place when sewing, you can refer back to the layout pattern you chose.

Example layout design
with 8 different fabrics

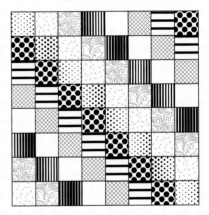

Example layout design
with 4 different fabrics

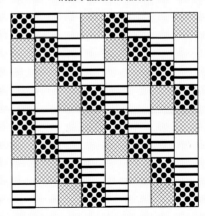

STEP 2: PIECE QUILT TOP

A   Starting with the top horizontal row, pin and sew all the squares **right** sides together, with a ¼-in/6-mm seam allowance. Press the seam allowances to the left. Return the completed strip of squares to the layout on the work surface.

B   Sew the second horizontal row of squares, **right** sides together, with a ¼-in/6-mm seam allowance. Press all the seam allowances to the right; return strip to layout on the work surface.

C   Repeat the above 2 steps until you have all of the squares sewn into 8 horizontal strips of 8 squares each, making sure that each strip has the seam allowance pressed in alternating directions (left, right, left, and so on). This will help reduce bulk and interlock each strip when they are sewn together. *(See illustration.)*

D   Pin the first 2 strips, **right** sides together, carefully matching each vertical seam between each square. Sew together with a ¼-in/6-mm seam allowance. Press seam down (toward the lower strip). Repeat, until all 8 strips are sewn together.

✻ PIECE QUILT TOP ✻
STEP **2C**

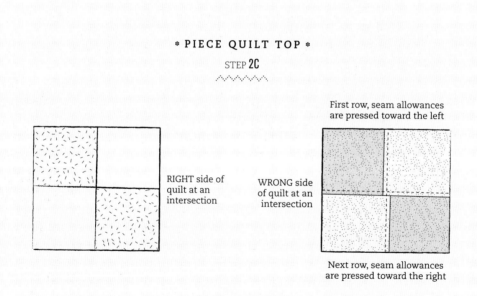

RIGHT side of quilt at an intersection

WRONG side of quilt at an intersection

First row, seam allowances are pressed toward the left

Next row, seam allowances are pressed toward the right

STEP 3: ASSEMBLE BACKING AND PREP FOR QUILTING.

A   Align Quilt Back pieces along the long edges, with **right** sides together; pin along one long edge. Sew pinned edges together with a ¼-in/6-mm seam allowance. Press seam allowance to one side. The Back should now be a 68-in/1.75-m square.

B   Lay Back flat on work surface, **right**-side down, and tape edges to surface with masking tape. Lay batting on top of Back, and trim batting to the same size as the Back. Smooth out any wrinkles, and then place the pieced Quilt Top, **right**-side up, centered on batting. Smooth out any wrinkles. The Quilt top will be about 3 to 4 in/7.5 to 10 cm smaller on all sides than the batting and Back.

C   Fold back the batting and pieced Top, so that the upper half of the **wrong** side of backing is visible. Spray backing and batting lightly with basting spray. Gradually roll the batting into place over the backing. Smooth out any wrinkles as necessary. Then lightly spray the batting and the **wrong** side of the pieced Quilt Top with basting spray. Gradually roll the Top into place over the batting. Smooth out any wrinkles. Repeat for lower half of Quilt. These 3 layers are now called the Quilt sandwich.

D   Starting from the center of the Quilt sandwich, either baste by hand, using needle and thread, or safety pin all three layers together.

STEP 4: FINISHING

A   Quilt the sandwiched layers together using your preferred method. To hand tie, see page 27. To stitch in the ditch, see page 27. To do free-motion quilting, see page 24. You can use one or a combination of these methods; it's up to you.

B   Cut off the excess batting and backing fabric, making sure that the corners are square and edges are straight.

C   *Binding:* Join the binding strips together, following instructions *(see page 22)*. Using an iron, press binding in half lengthwise, with **wrong** sides together, to make double-layer binding *(see page 22)*.

D   With Quilt **right**-side up, starting at the center of the lower edge of Quilt, align the binding raw edges with Quilt raw edge. Fold the end of the binding back 1 in/2.5 cm, and pin in place. Beginning at the folded end, sew the binding to the Quilt with a ¼-in/6-mm seam allowance. When you reach a corner, stop stitching and backstitch ½ in/12 mm from the corner. Take Quilt out from under presser foot, then rotate Quilt a quarter turn. Fold binding perpendicular to the seam, to create a diagonal fold, then fold the binding back down to align with the next Quilt raw edge. Make sure top folded edge of binding is aligned with the raw edges at the corner. Continue to sew the binding to the raw edge of the Quilt. This creates a mitered corner in the binding. Repeat at each corner of Quilt. When you reach the binding start point, overlap the end of binding over the folded back start point and stitch 1 in/2.5 cm beyond the folded edge at the starting point. *(See illustrations on page 146.)*

E Fold the binding over toward Back, encasing the raw edges. Pin in place, so that it covers the stitching from step 4D. Using needle and thread, slip stitch binding to Back. When you reach a corner, fold under the excess binding, to form a miter.

✳ FINISHING ✳
STEP 4D

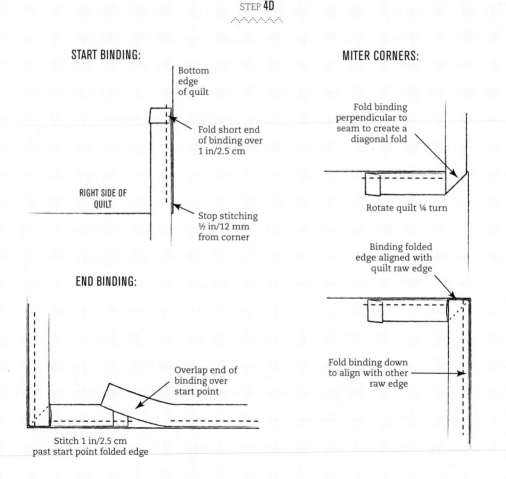

START BINDING:

Bottom edge of quilt

Fold short end of binding over 1 in/2.5 cm

RIGHT SIDE OF QUILT

Stop stitching ½ in/12 mm from corner

END BINDING:

Overlap end of binding over start point

Stitch 1 in/2.5 cm past start point folded edge

MITER CORNERS:

Fold binding perpendicular to seam to create a diagonal fold

Rotate quilt ¼ turn

Binding folded edge aligned with quilt raw edge

Fold binding down to align with other raw edge

• № 18 •

Olivia
Floral Lamp Shade

This floral lamp shade creates a romantic feel and casts
a gorgeous light. You can use vintage or new fabric roses,
but the more beautiful the flower, the more beautiful
the lamp. Use one type of flower or mix different
types of flowers with roses to create a varied look.
Use a 60-watt (or lower) lightbulb to keep
the glue from softening.

Materials

1 1 accent lamp with plain lamp shade

2 60 to 150 artificial flowers with leaves (the number of flowers will depend on size of lamp shade and size of flower heads)

FROM THE CRAFT CABINET:

❋ Hot-glue gun and glue sticks

Assemble

A Remove the flower heads and leaves from the stems of the flowers. Discard the stems.

B Work with the lamp shade on the lamp; this will make it easier to see how your work is progressing and how it looks with your lamp base. Using the hot-glue gun, attach the leaves to the top edge of the lamp shade, overlapping the ends of the leaves so the top edge is completely covered and the leaves wrap over the top edge to the inside of the lamp shade. Let glue dry. *(See illustration.)*

C Beginning at the bottom edge of the lamp shade, glue the flower heads in place. *(See illustration.)* Place them close together and work your way around the entire lower edge. Continue to glue the flower heads around the lamp shade, working from lower edge to top, until the entire lamp shade is completely covered. Let glue dry completely before turning on the lamp.

❋ **ASSEMBLE** ❋

STEPS **B** *and* **C**

Glue leaves to top edge; overlap ends of leaves to completely cover top edge.

Glue flower heads to bottom edge. Place them close together.

• № 19 •

Katie Eliza Canopy
and
Pinwheel Strands

In this feminine confection, yards of tulle and strands of pinwheel rosettes cascade down from a vintage carved cornice. You can find these vintage wooden window cornices at garage sales, flea markets, and even on eBay. Just add a bit of *Girl's World* flair, with some découpaged wallpaper or pretty paint, to make them special. If you can't find a vintage one, make one yourself, or have one made by someone with some woodworking skills and a jigsaw.

FINISHED SIZE OF CORNICE PICTURED (sizes may vary depending on the cornice you find)

❋ 42 in/107 cm wide by 9 in/23 cm high by 7 in/18 cm deep *(See illustration.)*

Materials

FOR CANOPY:

1 Remnant of wallpaper big enough to cover cornice front, sides, and top (Top is optional.)

2 1 vintage wooden window cornice

3 8 to 12 yd/7.5 to 11 m tulle fabric (Actual length of tulle will depend on how high the cornice is placed on the wall.)

4 Rolls of crepe paper (2 in/5 cm wide) in various colors

5 2 pieces craft felt (9 by 12 in/ 23 by 30.5 cm)

6 2 L-brackets, 4 in/10 cm

7 4 screws and bolts, to attach L-bracket to top of cornice

8 2 small swag hook screws (about 1½ in/ 4 cm in length)

9 4 screws, to attach L-bracket to wall (Use the correct type of screw for your type of wall.)

10 1 roll Hug Snug rayon seam binding (½ in/12 mm) (see "Resources," page 172)

11 1 to 2 sheets poster board (22 by 28 in/ 56 by 71 cm)

12 Fine glitter

FROM THE CRAFT CABINET:

❋ Pencil

❋ Scissors (for use with paper and fabric)

❋ Tape measure

❋ Newspapers to cover your work area

❋ Fine-grit sandpaper

❋ Cloth rag

❋ 4-in/10-cm sponge brush

❋ Mod Podge

❋ Power drill and drill bits

❋ Screwdriver

❋ White glue

❋ Hot-glue gun and glue sticks

Note: The cornice pictured on page 152 is made up of the decorative Front piece, a top piece, 2 side pieces, and some decorative molding around the top edges. There are no back or bottom pieces. The cornice is attached to the wall with L-brackets, mounted to the inside top piece.

WALLPAPER (TO COVER CORNICE):

Lay wallpaper remnant on flat surface with **right**-side down. Place Front of cornice on wallpaper and trace around the Front using a pencil. Draw 2 rectangles for the cornice sides (use the measurements of your cornice sides). Draw 1 rectangle for the cornice top (use the measurements of your cornice top); remember that the top piece is optional. Cut out all pieces.

TULLE FABRIC:

To get an accurate measurement of the tulle needed, hang the cornice and use a tape measure to determine the length from the inside swag hook down to the floor. Multiply that number by 4, then divide that number by 36 for yardage or 100 for meters. This will be the total length needed. For example, a measurement from the swag hook to floor of 72 in/183 cm multiplied by 4 equals 288 in/ 7.3 m. Divide this by 36 or 100. The total amount of tulle needed is 8 yd/7.3 m. Cut this total length in half, so you have 2 pieces that are 4 yd/3.75 m each.

CREPE PAPER (FOR PINWHEEL STRANDS):

Cut 1 piece of crepe paper for each pinwheel desired, in color(s) of your choice, each 1 by 36 in/ 2.5 by 91 cm.

FELT (FOR PINWHEELS):

Cut 1 circle from felt per pinwheel, each 2 in/5 cm in diameter.

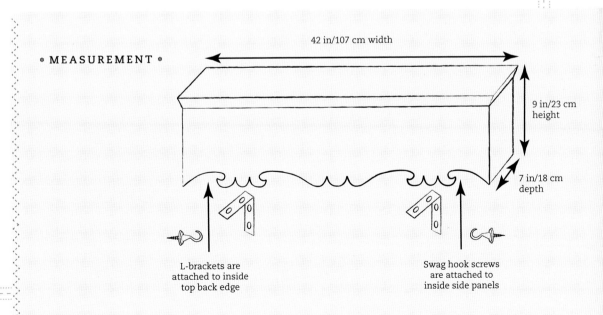

✴ MEASUREMENT ✴

42 in/107 cm width

9 in/23 cm height

7 in/18 cm depth

L-brackets are attached to inside top back edge

Swag hook screws are attached to inside side panels

STEP 1: CORNICE

A Cover your work surface with plenty of newspaper. Lightly sand the Cornice and wipe with a damp cloth to remove sanding dust.

B Using a sponge brush, coat the **wrong** side of the wallpaper and outside of Cornice with Mod Podge. Affix wallpaper pieces to Cornice. Let dry.

C Using a drill, drill holes through top of Cornice where the L-brackets will be placed. Attach brackets to inside top edge with screws and bolts.

D Using a drill, drill 1 small hole on the inside of each side panel on cornice, about 3 in/7.5 cm from the lower edge. Screw small swag screw into each of the holes.

E Hang the Cornice on the wall, by screwing the L-brackets to the wall.

F Fold 1 of the cut tulle pieces in half lengthwise. Cut about 18 in/46 cm of seam binding off the roll. Place the seam binding between the 2 layers of tulle at the fold and tie into a knot; this will gather up the tulle along the fold. Tie the seam binding to 1 of the inside swag hooks on the Cornice. Repeat on other side of Cornice with second piece of tulle.

❋ **PINWHEEL STRANDS** ❋

STEP **2A**

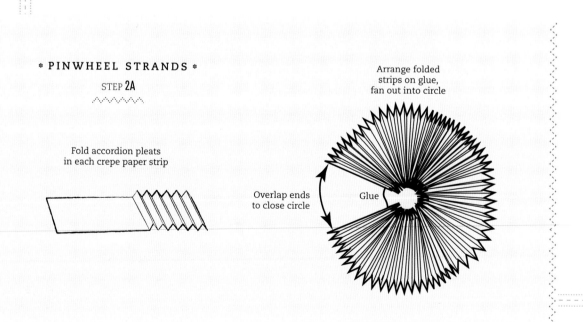

Fold accordion pleats in each crepe paper strip

Arrange folded strips on glue, fan out into circle

Overlap ends to close circle

Glue

STEP 2: PINWHEEL STRANDS

A Lay poster board on flat surface and place about a ¾-in/2-cm circle of white glue on it. Fold a crepe paper strip into small accordion pleats. Place 1 of the pleated edges on the circle of glue, fan out the accordion pleats to create a circle and overlap the 2 ends. Continue to glue the folded crepe paper to the same piece of poster board until you have folded all the crepe paper strips. If you run out of room, use the second sheet of poster board. *(See illustration.)*

B Add a little more white glue to the center of each circle and shake glitter over the centers of the circles. Shake off excess glitter and let the circles dry for 24 hours. Once dry, cut the circles out. You will want to cut the poster board backing slightly smaller than the crepe paper circles, so that it can't be seen when you are looking at the glittered side of the circles. These circles will now be referred to as the Pinwheels.

C *Pinwheel Strands:* (Make 3.) Unroll some of the seam binding and hot glue a felt circle about 18 in/46 cm from the end. Then glue a Pinwheel to the felt circle, sandwiching the seam binding between them. Continue to glue felt circles and Pinwheels to the seam binding, spacing them about 3 to 4 in/7.5 to 10 cm apart. Unroll the seam binding as needed until you reach the desired length of Pinwheel Strand. Make 1 Strand to tie to each swag hook and 1 to tie around the top of the Cornice. Let the Pinwheel Strands dry completely before tying them in place.

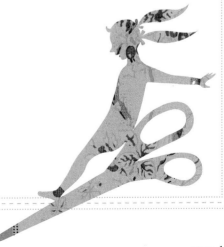

• № 20 •

Molly Patchwork Memory Board

Who says a bulletin board needs to be made of boring old cork? This project merges whimsy with function. Feel free to customize the board to your girl's particular taste. You can use a single piece of fabric for the background or create a simple patchwork design. Play around with the ribbon to create your own personalized look. This memory board project was contributed by Marnie Ruane, MRR Design.

FINISHED SIZE OF MEMORY BOARD ❋ 25 by 20 in/63.5 by 50 cm

Materials

1   20 assorted mid-weight cotton fabric scraps (each 7 by 7 in/18 by 18 cm) for randomly pieced patchwork background

OR

4 fat quarters (18 by 22 in/46 by 56 cm) of printed mid-weight cotton fabric for pieced patchwork background

OR

¾ yd/70 cm of printed mid-weight cotton fabric (45 in/114 cm wide) for solid piece background

2   Coordinating thread

3   25-by-20-in/63.5-by-50-cm cotton batting

4   25-by-20-in/63.5-by-50-cm Homasote fiberboard (see "Resources," page 172)

5   5 yd/4.5 m ribbon (½ in/12 mm wide)

6   13 decorative upholstery nails or tacks (each ⅜ in/1 cm)

7   25-by-20-in/63.5-by-50-cm sheet of paper (A heavyweight wrapping paper will work well.)

8   Picture-hanging kit (includes screw eyes, picture wire, picture hooks, and nails)

FROM THE SEWING BASKET:

❋ Scissors (for use with fabric)

❋ Rotary cutter and cutting mat (These are optional, but make cutting all those squares a lot easier.)

❋ Pins

❋ Clear ruler

FROM THE CRAFT CABINET:

❋ Digital camera or graph paper and colored pencils

❋ Staple gun and staples

❋ 2-in/5-cm sponge brush

❋ White glue

Note: You can make this memory board any size. Just be sure that the background fabric measures at least 2 in/5 cm larger on all sides than the fiberboard. Adjust size of batting, paper backing, and amount of ribbon accordingly.

Cutting

FOR PIECED FABRIC BACKGROUND:
Cut 20 squares, 6.5 in/16.5 cm each.

FOR SOLID PIECE FABRIC BACKGROUND:
Cut 1 rectangle, 24 by 29 in/61 by 74 cm, and skip to step 2.

Assemble

STEP 1: BACKGROUND

A Depending on how many fabrics you choose for the background, you need to decide on how you want the squares to be pieced together. We have provided an option for the layout, using 4 different fabrics. *(See illustration on page 162.)* This is just an idea; feel free to play with different layout patterns. *Note:* To try your own layout pattern, lay all of the squares for the Background on the floor or work table in a 4-by-5 grid, moving the squares around until you're happy with the overall layout pattern.

B Once you have the layout decided, take a quick picture or draw your layout pattern on a piece of graph paper with colored pencils; that way, if the squares get moved or you lose your place when sewing, you can refer back to the layout picture or graph paper.

C Beginning with the top horizontal row, sew all of the squares, **right** sides together, with a ¼-in/6-mm seam allowance. Press the seam allowances to the left. Return the completed strip of squares to the layout on the work surface.

D Sew the second horizontal row of squares, **right** sides together, with a ¼-in/6-mm seam allowance. Press all the seam allowances to the right; return strip to layout on the work surface.

E Continue the above 2 steps until you have all of the squares sewn into 5 horizontal strips, making sure that each strip has the seam allowance pressed in alternating directions (left, right, left). This will help reduce bulk and interlock each strip when they're sewn together *(see "Genevieve Patchwork Square Quilt" step 2C illustration on page 144)*.

F Pin the first 2 strips with **right** sides together, carefully matching each vertical seam between every square. Sew together with a ¼-in/6-mm seam allowance. Press seam down (toward the lower strip). Repeat, until all 5 strips are sewn together.

❋ BACKGROUND ❋

STEP 1A
∿∿∿∿∿∿∿

Example layout design
with 4 different fabrics

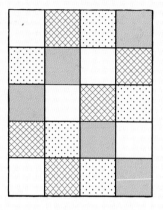

❋ COVER FIBERBOARD ❋

STEPS 2B *and* 2C
∿∿∿∿∿∿∿

Center fiberboard on WRONG side
of background fabric

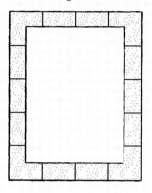

Fold long edge over fiberboard
and secure with staples

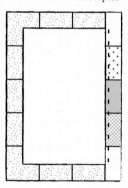

Fold corners over diagonally, then fold
over fiberboard and secure with staples

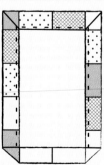

❋ RIBBON LAYOUT ❋

STEP 2D
∿∿∿∿∿∿∿

Place ribbon diagonally
from corner to corner

Then place
ribbon
diagonally
from center
point of
each side

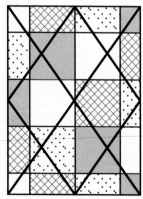

STEP 2: COVER FIBERBOARD

A Place batting on board, align all edges and secure in place with staples.

B Place Background fabric, **wrong**-side up, on a flat surface; place fiberboard, batting-side down, on top of Background fabric and center it on Background. Fold one long Background edge over the fiberboard and secure with staples. Fold the second long Background edge over the fiberboard, pull fabric slightly so it's taut, and secure with staples. *(See illustration.)*

C Fold top edge corners down (as you would when wrapping a present). Then fold top edge over fiberboard, pulling fabric slightly so it's taut, and secure with staples. *(See illustration.)* Repeat for bottom edge.

D Turn board **right**-side up. Attach Ribbon: Begin by placing ribbon diagonally, from corner to corner; wrap ribbon to the back of board, and staple in place. Repeat on other corners. Find the center point of the top edge and one side edge; place ribbon diagonally from each center point by wrapping ribbon to the back and stapling it in place. Repeat 3 more times so there are ribbons placed diagonally from each center point. *(See illustration.)*

E Insert a decorative upholstery nail or tack at each of the ribbon intersections and each corner.

F Turn Board **wrong**-side up. Using sponge brush, spread white glue evenly over back of board, coating ribbon ends and edges of fabric. Carefully place paper **right**-side up on the **wrong** side of board, aligning edges. Let dry.

G Follow instructions on picture-hanging kit to attach 2 screw eyes and picture wire across back of board. Then hang up on the wall.

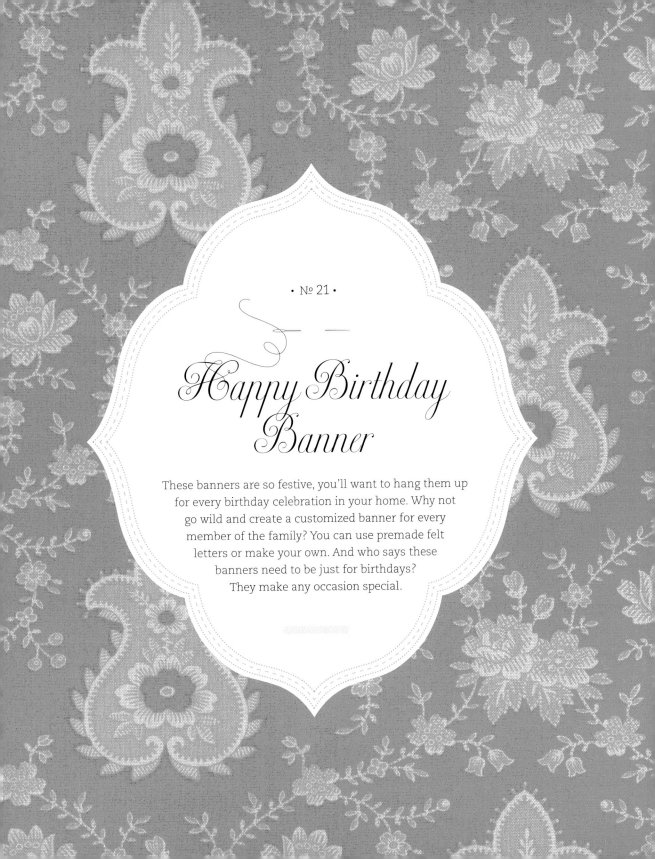

· № 21 ·

Happy Birthday Banner

These banners are so festive, you'll want to hang them up for every birthday celebration in your home. Why not go wild and create a customized banner for every member of the family? You can use premade felt letters or make your own. And who says these banners need to be just for birthdays? They make any occasion special.

FINISHED SIZE OF BANNER (including ties) ❀ 8 by 100 in/20 cm by 2.54 m

Materials

1 13 assorted mid-weight cotton scraps (each 8 by 6 in/20 by 15 cm), for Banner

2 ¼ yd/23 cm printed mid-weight cotton fabric (45 in/114 cm wide) for binding

3 ½ yd/45 cm fusible fleece (45 in/114 cm wide) for backing (we used Pellon Thermolam Plus)

4 2 yd/2 m pom-pom fringe ½ in/12 mm wide

5 1 package 2-in/5-cm self-adhesive felt letters (we used CPE Stick-It Felt Letters) or enough felt to make your own letters

6 Coordinating thread

FROM THE SEWING BASKET:

❀ Scissors (for use with fabric)

❀ Ruler

❀ Hand-sewing needle (optional)

❀ Water-soluble fabric marker or chalk pencil

❀ Pins

FROM THE CRAFT CABINET:

❀ Hot-glue gun and glue sticks (optional)

Cutting

FROM THE BANNER FABRICS:
Cut 13 rectangles, each 7 by 5 in/17 by 12 cm.

FROM THE BINDING FABRIC:
Cut enough 2-in-/5-cm-wide cross-grain binding strips *(see page 22)*, so that, when pieced together, they measure 100 in/2.54 m long.

FROM THE FUSIBLE FLEECE:
Cut 13 rectangles, each 7 by 5 in/17 by 12 cm.

FROM THE POM-POM FRINGE:
Cut 13 pieces, each 5 in/12 cm long.

Assemble

STEP 1: BANNER PIECES

A Lay fusible fleece backing pieces on a flat surface, with fusible side facing up; place fabric Banner pieces on top of each fleece piece, with **right** side facing up. Fuse pieces together, following fusible fleece manufacturer's instructions.

B Place fused Banner pieces on a flat surface and arrange them as desired. Center felt letters on each Banner piece. Follow felt letter manufacturer's instructions to adhere felt letters to Banner pieces. If letters don't bond firmly to the Banner pieces, tack them down either with sewing machine or by hand with a few backstitches using needle and thread. If you're making your own letters from felt, you can either sew or hot glue them to the Banner pieces.

C Attach pom-pom fringe to the front lower edge of each Banner piece, by sewing in place or using hot glue. If using hot glue, let it dry completely before proceeding to next step.

STEP 2: FINISHING

A Join the cross-grain binding strips together, following the instructions on page 22. Then press the joined strip into double-fold binding *(see page 20)*.

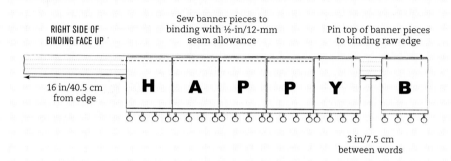

B Unfold binding entirely and place on flat surface with **right** side facing up. Using a ruler, measure in from each end 16 in/40.5 cm and make a mark with a fabric marker or chalk pencil on the top raw edge. With Banner pieces in the correct order, beginning at left mark, working from left to right, place them with **right** side facing up, on binding. Align the binding top raw edge with the top raw edge of the Banner pieces and pin them in place. The Banner pieces should be butted up against each other for each word; leave a 3-in/7.5-cm gap between the words. *(See illustration.)*

C Sew the Banner pieces to the binding with a ½-in/12-mm seam allowance. *(See illustration.)* Trim the seam allowance on the Banner piece to ⅛ in/3 mm.

D Fold the binding to the front of the Banner, enclosing all raw edges. Begin at one end and pin the binding folded edges together; then pin the binding to Banner pieces so it covers the stitching made in step 2C; at opposite end of binding, pin folded edges together. Sew the binding ⅛ in/3 mm from folded edge, along the entire length of the Banner. Press.

E Knot each end of the binding and you're ready to celebrate in style.

Resources

SEWING AND CRAFT SUPPLIES

CHIP BOARD

MAYA ROAD
Mayaroad.net

FABRIC AND NOTIONS

HART'S FABRIC
1620 Seabright Avenue
Santa Cruz, CA 95062
831 423 5434
Hartsfabric.com

*Assortment of cottons,
fashion, drapery, upholstery,
and eco fabrics, including
nylon tulle netting*

MAKE & MINGLE FABRIC STORE
63 Unquowa Road
Fairfield, CT 06824
203 292 8668
Makeandmingle.com

*Fabrics, embellishments,
and vintage finds*

TINSEL TRADING COMPANY
1 West 37th Street
New York, NY 10018
212 730 1030
Tinseltrading.com

*Wide range of high-quality notions
and sewing supplies, including metal fabrics,
fringes, and vintage flowers*

FASHION JEWELRY

VINTAGE JEWELRY
Ebay.com

WITCHYPOO ACCESSORIES
Witchypooaccessories.com

*Fashion jewelry and
other accessories*

FELT

CREATE FOR LESS
Createforless.com

*Complete source of craft
supplies, including CPE
Stick-It Felt Letters*

THE FELT PEOPLE
Thefeltpeople.com

*Felt supplies, including
felt for back of pinwheels*

FLOWERS

AFLORAL.COM
Silk flowers

ALDIK
7651 Sepulveda Boulevard
Van Nuys, CA 91405
818 988 5970
Aldikhome.com

Silk flowers and gifts

PETAL GARDEN
Petalgarden.com

*Silk- and freeze-dried
rose petals*

PETAL TOSS
Petaltoss.com

Rose petals

FUSIBLE FLEECE AND INTERFACINGS

HTC INC
888 275 4275
Htc-retail.com

*Ultrafirm nonwoven heavy-weight
sewing interfacing*

PELLON
Pellonideas.com

Interfacings and interlinings

HOMASOTE BOARD

HOME DEPOT
Homedepot.com

PAPER DOLLS

PAPER DOLL REVIEW
800 290 2928
Paperdollreview.com

Vintage paper doll reproductions

PILLOW INSERTS

AURORA PILLOW INSERTS
Aurorapillow.com

PILLOWFLEX, INC.
Pillowflex.com

*Polyester and latex pillows
and pillow forms*

POM-POMS

A TREASURE NEST
Atreasurenest.com

Craft supplies

RIBBON

BROWN PAPER PACKAGES
813 679 5546
Brownpaperpackages1.blogspot.com

Wonderful selection of vintage ribbon

KEL-TOY INC.
Keltoy.com

Great assortment of beautiful ribbon, including metallic (glitter) ribbon

RUFFLED BENCH
Bebepapillon.com

Papillon Linens

SEAM BINDING AND ZIPPERS

ZIPPERSTOP
Zipperstop.com

Hug Snug, seam binding ribbon, zippers, and other notions

THREAD

COATS AND CLARK
800 648 1479
Coatsandclark.com

Wide range of colorful yarns, threads, books, and supplies

WOOD CORNICES

WILTON WOODWORKING
203 762 7999

WHERE TO FIND SIS BOOM PRODUCTS AND FABRICS

PEKING HANDICRAFT
1388 San Mateo Avenue
South San Francisco, CA 94080
650 871 3788
Pkhc.com

For an assortment of Sis Boom product aprons, rugs, and pillows (wholesale)

SCIENTIFIC SEAMSTRESS
Scientificseamstress.com

Offers high-quality patterns and detailed sewing "protocols" in electronic format

SWAKEMBROIDERY.COM
SWAKembroidery.com

A good selection of machine embroidery designs, including Sis Boom motifs

WESTMINSTER FIBERS
Freespiritfabric.com
Westminsterfabrics.com

A huge assortment of designer fabrics

YOU CAN MAKE THIS
Youcanmakethis.com

A great source for patterns and instructions, including Sis Boom patterns available for instant download

Index

SIS BOOM
JENNIFER PAGANELLI

Sisboom@optonline.net

Sisboom.com

VISIT MY BLOG

Jenniferpaganelli.typepad.com
Share your work with us
Sis Boom Sightings
Post photos of your Sis Boom projects on
our Sis Boom Sightings group on Flickr.com.
We want to see them!

‿‿‿‿‿‿‿‿‿‿‿

CREDITS

Clothing Stylist: Ise White
Isewhite.com

Hair Stylist: Ronnie Stam
Kramerkramer.com

Photo Stylist and Home interior Stylist: Mary Tucciarone
Tuccboys@aol.com

Patterns, Instructions, and Illustrations: Dolin O'Shea
Lulubliss.com

Pattern Testing: Carla Hageman Crim
Scientificseamstress.com

Photography: Tim Geaney
Timgeaney.com

Producer: Nicole Esposito Polly
Nicolepolly.com

Quilt Design and Airstream Stylist: Nancy DeWeir Geaney
of Dark Horse Farms Design
Darkhorsefarmdesigns.com

Upholstery: Maritza Bermudez of Frama Sewing
Framasewing.blogspot.com